VALUE ADDED TAX:
TWO VIEWS

VALUE ADDED TAX: TWO VIEWS

Charles E. McLure, Jr.
Norman B. Ture

American Enterprise Institute for Public Policy Research
Washington, D.C.

Charles E. McLure, Jr., is professor of economics at Rice University. Norman B. Ture is president of Norman B. Ture, Inc., an economic consulting firm in Washington, D.C.

Domestic Affairs Study 7, November 1972
Library of Congress Catalog Card No. L.C. 72-93448

Printed in United States of America

CONTENTS

THE TAX ON VALUE ADDED: PROS AND CONS

Charles E. McLure, Jr.

Summary and Conclusions

When it was rumored in early 1972 that President Nixon might propose a federal value added tax (VAT), interest in this form of taxation spread from the tax specialist to the congressman, newsman, and layman. Yet altogether too little material was available for the interested nonspecialist since most of the existing literature about the VAT had been written by experts in taxation for their fellow experts. This essay is intended to fill this gap by explaining what the value added tax is, how it operates, and the chief economic effects (and therefore advantages and disadvantages) of substituting revenues from a newly enacted VAT for part of the revenues from existing taxes.

A conscious attempt has been made to present the analysis in terms comprehensible to the educated layman—something always difficult to achieve for an inherently complex and technical matter. Because that effort may have fallen short of the mark and because some readers may simply not want to know as much about the value added tax as is presented in the body of the essay, the most important points are summarized in the next few pages. Footnotes in the summary refer to relevant portions of the text itself.

The term "tax on value added" is at once quite descriptive and highly misleading. It describes well the way in which the tax is collected. Each firm pays a tax on the increase in the value of goods that occurs because of the firm's productive activities; hence the term

1

"tax on value added."[1] If the tax is levied on all firms in the productive process, including retailers, it will be collected upon the total value of the final product. Thus in its pure form the tax is essentially equivalent to a general single-stage sales tax levied at the retail level.[2] In this sense the value added tax is not a tax on some new and different tax base; it is simply a different way of collecting a general tax on consumption.

Because the VAT is intended to be a tax on all domestic consumption, it is necessary to make what are called border tax adjustments (BTA) on goods entering international trade. In other words, in order that exports not be burdened by the domestic tax on consumption, it is necessary to rebate any VAT previously collected on exports. Similarly, in order that imports bear the same tax as domestic consumption goods, it is necessary to apply the tax to them. These border tax adjustments are among the most famous characteristics of the VAT. (It is worthwhile to note that under a retail sales tax border tax adjustments are unnecessary; exports would have incurred no tax, and imports, like domestic products, would be taxed at the retail level.)[3]

Because it would ideally be levied at a uniform rate on all items of consumption, the VAT is said to be neutral. It does not distort economic decisions among products or methods of production. In this sense it is similar to the personal income and social security payroll taxes and quite different from the corporation income and property taxes. The corporation income tax, for which the VAT has most commonly been proposed as a substitute, is distinctly nonneutral. It discriminates against the products of the corporate sector, against the use of the corporate form of business organization, against the use of equity (share) financing in the corporate sector, and against the use of capital (as opposed to land and labor) in the corporate sector. Thus, partial replacement of the corporation income tax with a truly general tax on value added (one with few exemptions and a uniform rate)

---

[1] In actuality, in all nations now using the tax the firm incurs a tax liability equal to the tax rate applied to the value of its sales, but receives credit for taxes it has paid on its purchased inputs. As discussed further in section 2C of the essay, this *credit method* of taxation yields essentially the same results as applying the tax rate directly to value added.

[2] These statements are strictly true only for the consumption type VAT, the variant most likely to be adopted in the United States. See section 2B for a description of the income and consumption variants of the VAT.

[3] See section 2E for a detailed discussion of border tax adjustments.

would represent a distinct gain in neutrality, provided it were accompanied by increased taxation of retained earnings.[4]

A similar, if less dramatic, increase in neutrality would result from using revenues from a general VAT to replace part of the revenues from local school property taxes, the scheme President Nixon has proposed for consideration. The property tax, as it now operates, distorts intra-urban choices of industrial location and retards the renewal of decaying central cities. Partial replacement of the property tax on improvements with a neutral VAT would reduce these distortions.

Only a truly general VAT would be completely neutral. If the tax contained important exemptions or if it were applied to different products at different rates, its inherent neutrality would be lost. For this reason exemptions should be kept to a minimum and a single rate should be applied to all products. Nevertheless, it is virtually certain that an American VAT would contain important exemptions. For one thing, it is very difficult to tax housing and the output of financial institutions under the VAT. If only these and several other difficult-to-tax items were exempted, the tax base would fall to about 80 percent of personal consumption expenditures. Moreover, several items of expenditure might be thought worthy of exemption as a matter of social policy. Examples are medicine and medical expenses, public education and research expenditures, and religious and welfare activities. Exemptions of this type might reduce the tax base further, to only about two-thirds of personal consumption expenditures. Finally, such things as household utilities and food for home preparation might be exempted in order to lessen the regressivity of the tax. If so, the tax base would fall to less than one-half of personal consumption expenditures.[5] Exemptions of this size would, of course, render the VAT far from the neutral fiscal device that it is in its pure form. One of the most important ways to forestall the erosion of the tax base and maintain neutrality would be to offset the regressivity of the VAT through refundable credits against the income tax or a negative income tax, rather than through the exemption of necessities. This is discussed further below.

---

[4] Simple elimination of a part of the corporation income tax would partially free retained earnings from taxation. Retained earnings could be taxed via increased capital gains taxation or the integration of the two income taxes (attributing all corporate profits to shareholders and including them in personal income tax returns); see section 4B.

[5] See section 3 for a more detailed description of the potential erosion of the ideally neutral tax base.

Assessment of most of the effects of replacing part of the corporation income tax with a levy on value added hinges crucially upon one of the most controversial issues in economics, the incidence of the corporation income tax.[6] Traditional economic theory states that the corporation income tax cannot be shifted to consumers in the form of higher product prices or to labor (or suppliers) in the form of lower wages (or input prices); rather, it must be borne by shareholders in the form of reduced earnings. Other theoretical analyses and certain controversial empirical studies report quite different results, namely, that the corporation income tax can be and is shifted. Thus the best that can be done is to make conditional statements. *If* the corporation tax is shifted to consumers, it probably has about the same effects in the aggregate as the VAT or any other general consumption tax. *If* it is not shifted, but is borne by shareholders, the result is quite different. In what follows we summarize the likely results of replacing part of the corporation income tax with a VAT under both sets of assumptions about shifting.

If the corporation tax is not shifted, the rate of saving and investment in the economy would probably rise markedly if the VAT were substituted for the corporation tax. Presumably this change would raise the rate of growth in the United States. But if the corporation tax is shifted, probably little impact on the rates of saving, investment, and growth would occur. If the VAT were substituted for the personal income tax, social security payroll tax, or property tax, the impact on these rates would probably also be small.

Evidence from the 1968 income tax surcharge suggests that temporary changes in income tax rates are not strong tools of discretionary counter-cyclical policy. The same conclusion probably would hold for the payroll tax. Thus the VAT might be a more useful tool of discretionary fiscal policy than any of these direct taxes, since temporary changes in it would be likely to cause consumers to accelerate or postpone purchases of durable goods at just the right times. Of course, we do not expect the property tax to be varied as a tool of stabilization policy. So far as contribution to the built-in stability of the economy is concerned, it seems unlikely that the various taxes differ significantly.

---

[6] See section 4A for a brief discussion of the incidence of the corporation income tax. The remainder of section 4 considers in detail the implications for neutrality, growth, stabilization, and the balance of payments of substituting a VAT for the corporation income tax. Distributional effects of the substitution are left for section 5. Each of these effects is discussed for the substitution of VAT for the personal income and payroll taxes in section 6 and for the substitution for the property tax in section 7.

Perhaps the most important way in which the VAT would differ from the income taxes is in its incidence. The VAT, being a tax on consumption, would almost certainly be markedly regressive since consumption as a percentage of income falls as income rises. On the other hand, the personal and corporate income taxes are progressive (if the corporate tax is not shifted; if the corporate tax is shifted, it too is regressive). Thus substitution of VAT for part of either of these taxes is felt by many observers to be grossly inequitable. They would oppose substitution for the personal tax and would favor substitution for the corporate tax only if the change were accompanied by heavier taxation of capital gains and relief for low-income families. This relief ideally would take the form of a refundable income tax credit or a negative income tax, but some would accept exemption of necessities such as food from the tax base. Such exemptions would, as noted above, be a distinctly inferior form of relief because they would destroy the neutrality of the VAT, one of the chief advantages of the tax in its pure form.

Perhaps the most widely advertised of the supposed advantages of an American switch to the VAT is an expected improvement in the balance of payments. In its simplest form this argument is probably fallacious; it simply states that, because border tax adjustments are allowed for the VAT, exports would increase and imports would fall. The problem with this view is that the BTA are seen as import taxes and export subsidies, without recognizing that, as noted above, they would be needed to assure that the American tax is applied to all domestic consumption and that exports occur free of the tax. The fallacy in the argument is easily seen if we try to apply the same reasoning to the economically equivalent retail sales tax; hardly anyone would argue that imposition of that tax would, per se, improve the balance of trade. Only if the prices of goods failed to reflect fully either the retail tax or the VAT would the tax itself improve the payments position. Theoretical reasoning suggests that the VAT probably would raise prices by the amount of the tax, so there seems to be little reason for hope of balance of payments improvement on that score.

The real possibility of a switch to VAT improving the balance of payments arises, instead, from the assumption that the corporation income tax is shifted. Traditional theory holds that the corporation tax is borne by shareholders, and thus has no effect on prices. Reduction of the tax would therefore not affect prices, and the switch to VAT would improve the balance of trade only if prices failed to rise by the amount of the newly imposed tax. On the other hand, if the corporation income tax is currently shifted to consumers, it resembles a sales tax except that no BTA is allowed for it. Thus the switch to VAT would have no effect on domestic prices (so long as the corporation tax is "unshifted" when reduced) but imports would be subject to the compensating import duty under the VAT and the tax rebated on exports. This result should, of course, improve the balance of payments.

What can we conclude about the effect of the switch on domestic prices and the balance of payments? Unfortunately, the answer is that we cannot conclude anything very firmly because we do not know whether or not the corporation income tax is shifted. But on balance it seems likely that domestic prices would rise by about the amount of the tax and that the balance of payments probably would not improve significantly if VAT were substituted for part of the corporation income tax. This conclusion is almost certainly accurate if the VAT were substituted instead for part of the personal income, payroll, or property tax.

Arguments with regard to neutrality, equity, stability, growth, and the balance of payments have been summarized here. It is reasonable to ask how the various effects should be weighed since they do not all point together toward one single optimum direction for tax policy. The answer is clear: primary attention should be devoted to the implications for neutrality and equity. There are other tools, though imperfect ones, for the achievement of economic growth, stability, and an improved balance of payments; but neutrality in the tax system and equity in the distribution of tax burdens among households cannot very well be handled except through structural tax policy.[7]

If this reasoning is accepted, several conclusions stand out. First, if the corporation income tax is shifted to consumers, VAT should be substituted for it. Neutrality would be improved, with no substantial change in the equity of the tax system. But if the corporation income tax is not shifted, the trade-off between neutrality and equity must be faced squarely. The VAT is more neutral than the corporation tax, but it is also regressive. Of course, if the tax haven in the form of retained earnings, which would be created by reduction of the corporation tax, were closed, both neutrality and equity would be furthered. But it is virtually certain that relief from the regressivity of the VAT would need to be provided for low-income families. In the interest of maintaining neutrality, this relief should be provided

---

[7] This argument is presented in more detail in section 9.

directly through refundable credits or a negative income tax rather than through exemption of necessities from the VAT.

The choice between the VAT and the property tax is similar to that between the VAT and a shifted corporation tax. Neutrality would probably be increased while the overall incidence of the tax system probably would not change much. But housing might very well be exempt from the VAT, whereas it is currently taxed quite heavily under the property tax. The substitution of VAT for part of the personal income tax, on the other hand, would seem to make little sense. It would move the tax system toward regressivity and improve neutrality very little. Substitution for the payroll tax might be more or less a matter of indifference. Neutrality would be similar under both taxes, as would the aggregate distribution of burdens. But the VAT would bear more heavily on consumers, as a group, relative to workers, as a group.

Since administration of the VAT seems to be more involved than administration of the economically equivalent retail sales tax, it might reasonably be asked why there is so much interest in a federal VAT in preference to a federal retail sales tax. The answer is partly a matter of historical accident. France has used a form of value added tax since 1954, and since 1967 a dozen European countries have adopted, or have made arrangements to adopt, a VAT. The mystique of a tax used increasingly in Europe and largely unknown in the United States and the belief in some quarters that the U.S. balance of payments would be improved by adoption of a value added tax probably go a long way in explaining U.S. interest in the tax. The merit of these arguments for VAT deserves brief attention.

The European countries adopted value added taxes for reasons that are largely irrelevant to the United States. First, in many instances the VAT replaced what are known as cascade-type turnover taxes. These taxes apply to the entire value of a firm's sales at every transaction rather than to value added, and discriminate severely between products and methods of production, whereas a VAT is neutral with regard to both products and methods of production.[8] Second, the border tax adjustments that can be made precisely for the VAT can be made only roughly for cascade taxes. Third, and perhaps most important in European decisions to switch to value added taxation, the members of the European Common Market desired to harmonize their systems of indirect (consumption) taxation, something that could be achieved relatively easily under a VAT, but not under a regime of

---

[8] See section 2A for a more complete description of cascade taxes and their faults.

cascade taxation. Finally, because of the way it is administered, the VAT has self-enforcing features not shared by the cascade tax and many others.

None of these reasons for the European adoption of value added taxation is compelling in the United States. The United States, having no defective indirect tax such as the European cascade tax, need not impose a VAT to replace such a tax. And it is generally assumed that the level of taxpayer compliance in the United States is much higher than in Europe, and high enough to make the self-enforcement features of the VAT relatively unimportant. Finally, we have argued above that the switch to VAT probably would not improve the U.S. balance of payments very much, and that a switch to a retail sales tax would probably have roughly the same effect in any case. There are good reasons for preferring a value added tax to a retail tax, if either is to be adopted (and good reasons for preferences to run the other direction, as well), but neither the European precedent nor the balance of payments argument is among them.[9] Thus if some form of general sales tax is to be adopted, the VAT should not be chosen over the retail sales tax without a careful comparison of the relative administrative advantages of the two taxes.

1. Introduction

During the last ten years an increasingly popular topic in the world of fiscal affairs has been whether or not the United States should adopt a tax on value added (VAT).[10] The discussion began in earnest at about the time the Neumark committee recommended that all countries of the European Common Market should adopt a value added tax, and it intensified as that recommendation was implemented.[11] It

---

[9] See section 2F for a presentation of arguments on both sides of this issue.

[10] I defer to the judgment of readers of an earlier draft of this essay in using the abbreviation "VAT," rather than "TVA." I base my personal preference for the latter usage upon the grammatical superiority of "tax on value added," over "value added tax" and the prior use of TVA by the French—long before the United States seriously considered using the tax. Fortunately the French language does not readily admit such grammatical monstrosities as "value added tax."

[11] "Report of the Fiscal and Financial Committee (Neumark Report)," *The EEC Reports on Tax Harmonization*, International Bureau of Fiscal Documentation, Amsterdam, 1963. Thus far only the initial stages of the recommended changes have been completed. That is, all the countries of the EEC except Italy have adopted a VAT. The further stages of adoption of uniform rates and the origin principle with regard to trade internal to the EEC (see section 2E below) have yet to be implemented.

reached a crescendo recently when President Nixon suggested that the United States consider levying a federal VAT in order to lighten the burden of the property tax in the financing of education.

It seems accurate to say that support for an American VAT has been based in part upon a mystique derived jointly from the novelty of the idea and the fact that the Europeans are placing increasing reliance upon the tax and in part upon the improvement in the U.S. balance of payments that some persons thought the tax would produce, especially if it were substituted for part of the corporation income tax. In some quarters the neutrality of the VAT has been touted, as has its potential contribution to the rate of economic growth in the U.S.[12]

Critics of the VAT have decried the bandwagon effect that the VAT's mystique has seemed to create and have doubted that the balance-of-payments effects would be nearly as large as its supporters think. Moreover, they have argued that equilibrium in the balance of payments and a higher rate of economic growth could be achieved without such a radical change in tax policy. And while they have been willing to admit the neutrality of the VAT, if it were not riddled by exemptions, they have opposed imposing a regressive federal tax on consumption in the absence of income tax reform and low-income relief. It would be especially inequitable, some have argued, to substitute the regressive VAT for the progressive corporation income tax. Finally, even if the case were granted that the U.S. should have a broad-based federal tax on consumption, many have claimed that the more familiar retail sales tax would be preferable to the economically equivalent tax on value added.[13]

The purpose of this study is to present the arguments on both sides of the VAT question in a balanced and objective manner, so that the reader can decide for himself whether or not the U.S. should adopt a tax on value added. It proceeds by explaining in the next section

---

[12] In addition, the state of Michigan for a while had a quite imperfect variant of a tax on value added, the business activities tax (by coincidence, BAT). For two quite different assessments of the experience under this tax, see James A. Papke, "Michigan's Value-Added Tax after Seven Years," *National Tax Journal*, December 1960, pp. 350-63 and Clara K. Sullivan, *The Tax on Value Added* (New York: Columbia University Press, 1965), pp. 298-311.

[13] For a recent exchange on the merits and demerits of the VAT, see Stanley S. Surrey, "Value Added Tax: The Case For," and Dan Throop Smith, ". . . The Case Against," *Harvard Business Review*, December 1970, pp. 77-94. The present author has also examined the issues in "The Economic Effects of Taxing Value Added," mimeographed, 1970. His own views are expressed in testimony given before the Joint Economic Committee on March 21, 1972 and in the concluding section of this essay.

how the VAT is administered, important technical questions of the definition of the tax base for a general VAT applied without exemptions, and how the tax differs from a general retail sales tax in its administration. Section 3 examines the tax base as it would probably be in reality, i.e., given the seemingly irresistible tendency for any ideal tax base to be eroded by tax preferences and exemptions.

Whereas sections 2 and 3 discuss essentially the VAT itself (the comparison with the economically equivalent retail sales tax in section 2 being made primarily to clarify the operation of the VAT and to establish whether or not it is administratively preferable to a retail sales tax), the remainder of the study compares the VAT with other, quite different, taxes. In particular, section 4 compares the VAT and the corporation income tax with regard to neutrality, the effect on the rate of economic growth, use as macroeconomic stabilizers, and the impact on the U.S. balance of payments, while section 5 compares the incidence or distributional implications of the two taxes. The study, like most of the discussion in the last decade, concentrates on the comparison of these two taxes. For the sake of completeness the same comparison with the payroll and the personal incomes taxes is made in section 6.

Section 7 examines briefly the Nixon suggestion that a federal VAT might be substituted for the local property tax as a means of financing education. The analysis is done in the same terms as that of substituting VAT for the corporation income tax. But the Nixon proposal involves serious questions of fiscal relations between levels of government. Thus any meaningful analysis must go beyond these simple comparisons. Section 8 summarizes briefly European experience with the VAT, especially with regard to rate structure, coverage of the tax, and the impact on the price level of the introduction of the value added tax. The final section brings together the main points of the study, describes what the author believes is the proper framework for considering a tax on value added, and summarizes the author's views on the policy issues raised in this essay.

2. The Tax Base: Theory [14]

Though it is not strictly true, as is explained further in this and the next section, value added taxation can conveniently be envisaged as a means for collecting a general tax on consumer goods (and services)

---

[14] For a detailed exposition of the administration of value added taxes, see Carl S. Shoup, *Public Finance* (Chicago: Aldine Publishing Co., Inc., 1969), pp. 250-64.

as they pass through the stages of the production process, rather than entirely on the final sale to consumers, as under a retail sales tax. An example will make this clear. Assume that production involves three stages (A, B, and C) and that in a given taxable period production and transactions are as shown in Table 1 below. Firms at stage B buy inputs from those at stage A and sell their output to firms at stage C, which in turn sell only to ultimate consumers.[15]

Table 1
THREE-STAGE EXAMPLE OF 10 PERCENT VALUE ADDED TAX

| | Stage of Production | | | |
	A	B	C	Total
1. Sales	$300	$700	$1,000	$2,000
2. Purchased inputs	—	300	700	1,000
3. Value added (1 – 2)	300	400	300	1,000
4. Tax on value added (10% of 3)	30	40	30	100
5. Retail sales tax (10% of C1)	—	—	100	100

Under a 10 percent retail sales tax, $100 in revenue would be obtained on the $1,000 of sales made to consumers at stage C, as indicated. The same amount of revenue would be collected under the value added tax, but in an administratively different way. Each firm would be taxed at the 10 percent rate on its contribution to the value of the final product, or value added, which can be measured by the difference between its sales and its purchases of inputs. Thus firms at the three stages would pay VAT of $30, $40, and $30, respectively, on their value added of $300, $400, and $300. The total of VAT payments would, of course, equal the $100 collected directly on sales to consumers under the retail sales tax. The advantages and disadvantages of collecting the tax in this way, rather than simply at the retail level, are discussed in section 2F below, after further explanation of the operational details of the tax.

A.   Cascade Taxes and VAT Compared. It may be worthwhile at this point to digress momentarily to examine the difference between the value added tax and the gross turnover, or cascade, taxes being replaced by the VAT in Europe. Table 2 will help clarify the distinc-

---

[15] No distinction is made at this point between inputs of intermediate goods and capital goods. For a detailed discussion of the difference in treatment accorded them, see section 2B below.

Table 2

THREE-INDUSTRY COMPARISON OF 10 PERCENT VAT AND 5 PERCENT GROSS TURNOVER TAX

	Stage of Production			
	A	B	C	Total
Industry I (from Table 1)				
Sales	$300	$700	$1,000	$2,000
Purchased inputs	—	300	700	1,000
Value added	300	400	300	1,000
Value added tax	30	40	30	100
Retail sales tax	—	—	100	100
Gross turnover tax	15	35	50	100
Industry II				
Sales	—	—	1,000	1,000
Purchased inputs	—	—	—	—
Value added	—	—	1,000	1,000
Value added tax	—	—	100	100
Retail sales tax	—	—	100	100
Gross turnover tax	—	—	50	50
Industry III				
Sales	800	900	1,000	2,700
Purchased inputs	—	800	900	1,700
Value added	800	100	100	1,000
Value added tax	80	10	10	100
Retail sales tax	—	—	100	100
Gross turnover tax	40	45	50	135

tion between the VAT, a tax on net accretions of value, and the tax on gross sales. It shows the turnover tax liabilities that would be incurred by three hypothetical industries, each producing $1,000 of value added, if a cascade type tax were levied on gross sales at a rate of 5 percent. Industry I is repeated from Table 1 to give us a benchmark for comparison. Industry II is completely integrated, so that there is only one stage in the productive process. Finally, industry III has three stages, like industry I, but the split of value added by stages is quite different.

Because gross sales in industry I total $2,000, the 5 percent turnover tax on gross sales yields the same revenue as the 10 percent tax on value added, $100.[16] But the sales of the vertically integrated

---

[16] This example is inaccurate in one respect. The tax at any stage would be incorporated in the price of the taxed good. Thus the tax at the next stage would be applied to the gross price, including taxes paid at earlier stages. This aspect of taxing previous taxes is much less important than the multiple taxation of value added as it moves through the production process.

industry II are entirely to ultimate consumers, so that gross sales equal the value added of $1,000. Thus in this industry the 5 percent turnover tax yields but half the revenue of the 10 percent tax on value added. Whereas either the VAT or the retail sales tax would impose the same percentage tax burden on the products of the two industries, the turnover tax discriminates in favor of vertically integrated industries (and production processes).

Industry III has the same number of stages as industry I. But because value added occurs earlier in the production process and is subjected to the turnover tax repeatedly as it moves through later stages, total sales of the industry are greater than for industry I. Thus, in total, the industry bears a $135 tax burden rather than the $100 burden on industry I. As a rule the turnover tax discriminates against industries whose value added occurs early in the production process.

It was because of the distortions created in the domestic economies by this nonneutral tax (plus the difficulties in calculating border tax adjustments, mentioned in footnote 27 of this section) that the Neumark Report recommended that the cascade type turnover taxes be replaced by the nondistorting tax on value added.[17] Because of the discrimination inherent in it, the cascade type turnover tax is a decidedly inferior form of taxation.

B. Income and Consumption Type VAT. The above example of computing the tax base under a value added tax ignored the question of how capital goods should be treated in the computation. For convenience we simply assumed implicitly that there were no capital goods. To make the example more realistic and more informative, we now consider explicitly the tax treatment of capital goods.

The two alternatives that are relevant in the present discussion are the income and consumption varieties of VAT.[18] Under the consumption variety, purchases of capital goods, as well as intermediate goods, are offset immediately against gross sales in computing taxable value added. Thus, there is no need to distinguish between the two types of business purchases, and the example in Table 1 is directly applicable.

Under the income type VAT, only depreciation on capital goods (as well as purchases of intermediate goods), rather than the entire

---

[17] For a further discussion of neutrality and tax-induced distortions, see section 4 below.

[18] See Shoup, *Public Finance*, pp. 251-53 for a description of the gross product and wage type value added taxes.

purchase price in the period of acquisition, can be offset against sales. Thus capital goods must be distinguished from intermediate goods, and depreciation schedules for tax purposes must be established for the former. Table 3 gives an example of the calculation of value added under the income type VAT, and compares it with the calculation under the consumption variety.

Table 3

COMPARISON OF INCOME AND CONSUMPTION TYPE TAXES ON VALUE ADDED

	Stage of Production			Total Economy
	A	B	C	
1. Sales	$300	$700	$1,000	$2,000
a. Intermediate goods	300	500	—	800
b. Capital goods	—	200	—	200
c. Consumer goods	—	—	1,000	1,000
2. Purchased inputs				
a. Intermediate goods	—	300	500	800
b. Capital goods	—	—	200	200
3. Capital stock				
a. Initial (assumed)	800	1,000	1,200	3,000
b. Purchases of capital goods (2b)	—	—	200	200
c. Depreciation (.05 × (3a + 3b))	40	50	70	160
d. End of period (3a + 3b − 3c)	760	950	1,330	3,040
e. Net investment (3d − 3a)	−40	−50	130	40
4. Value added				
a. Income base (1 − 2a − 3c)	260	350	430	1,040
b. Consumption base (1 − 2a − 2b)	300	400	300	1,000
5. Factor payments plus net profits				
a. Wages	160	220	300	680
b. Rent	40	30	20	90
c. Interest	30	50	60	140
d. Net profit	30	50	50	130
e. Total	260	350	430	1,040

Because purchases of both intermediate goods and capital goods are offset immediately against sales under the consumption type VAT, the net tax base equals sales of final products to ultimate consumers, or consumption. Thus it is equal to the base of an ideal retail sales tax, that is, of a single-stage sales tax applied only to sales to final consumers.

On the other hand, the tax base under the income type VAT equals income, rather than consumption, since for capital goods only depreciation is allowed as an offset against sales. This distinction can be seen in Table 3 by noting that value added under the income type VAT equals the sum of factor payments and net profits. For this reason a value added tax of the income variety is equivalent to a flat rate personal income tax with no exemptions or deductions. Of course, the base of the income type VAT exceeds that of the consumption type by the amount of net investment. Because the base for a VAT would be income or consumption, and not some new or different tax base, it is proper to think of the value added tax as an administrative device for collecting a tax on one of these bases rather than as a wholly new tax.

In most of what follows, especially in sections 4 to 7, attention focuses upon the consumption type tax because it is the most likely to be adopted in the United States. This likelihood is attributable to several factors. First, the consumption type VAT is used in Europe, and pressure to use it here would be strong. Second, the treatment of capital goods is far simpler than under the income type tax, which would require depreciation schedules and accounting. Finally, an additional tax on income could far more easily be implemented directly, by adding several points to the personal income tax rates, rather than by imposing an income type tax on value added.

C. **Calculating Tax Liabilities.** Section B above described in general terms the calculation of value added under the income and consumption varieties of value added tax. It may be useful, however, to describe in greater detail several alternative accounting techniques for computing tax liabilities. This detail will enable us to understand better the administrative advantages and disadvantages of the VAT, relative to the retail sales tax, which are discussed in section 2F.

The two most straightforward methods of calculating tax liabilities under the VAT are variants of what can be called the deduction method. Under the first, the subtraction method, the statutory tax rate is applied directly to the firm's value added, which in turn is calculated by subtracting purchased inputs from sales. Under the consumption type VAT, immediate deduction is made for purchases of both intermediate and capital goods, whereas under the income variety deduction for capital goods is allowed only as the assets depreciate. Thus, Table 4 shows the tax liabilities that would result from a 10 percent tax and the transactions and production indicated in Table 3. Total tax liabilities under the consumption type tax would

Table 4

COMPARISON OF THREE METHODS OF CALCULATING LIABILITIES UNDER VALUE ADDED TAXATION

	Stage of Production			Total Economy
	A	B	C	
1. Subtraction method:				
a. Value added (from Table 3)				
1. Consumption base	$300	$400	$ 300	$1,000
2. Income base	260	350	430	1,040
b. Tax liability at 10% rate				
1. Consumption base	30	40	30	100
2. Income base	26	35	43	104
2. Credit method:				
a. Sales (from Table 3)	300	700	1,000	2,000
b. Purchases (from Table 3)				
1. Intermediate goods	—	300	500	800
2. Capital goods	—	—	200	200
c. Depreciation (from Table 3)	40	50	70	160
d. Gross tax liability on sales, at 10% rate	30	70	100	200
e. Tax on purchases and depreciation at 10% rate				
1. Consumption base (10% of b1+b2)	—	30	70	100
2. Income base (10% of b1+c)	4	35	57	96
f. Net tax liability				
1. Consumption base (d−e1)	30	40	30	100
2. Income base (d−e2)	26	35	43	104
3. Addition method:				
a. Sum of factor payments and profits (from Table 3)	260	350	430	1,040
b. Tax liability at 10% rate (income base only)	26	35	43	104

be 10 percent of sales to consumers, while under the income type tax they would be 10 percent of income; in either case the tax would be collected as the goods moved through the production process.

Under the second variant of the deduction method the firm calculates its gross tax liability by applying the statutory rate to its total sales. It then deducts from the result the amount of tax it has paid on its purchases in order to calculate its net tax liability. Because credit is allowed for the taxes previously paid on inputs, this method of calculating tax liability is known as the credit method. Of course, under the income type VAT, credit can be taken for taxes paid on capital goods only as the assets depreciate, whereas under the consumption type tax, credit is allowed for the total tax immediately. Table 4 also shows calculations of tax liabilities under the credit method. Liabilities are, of course, the same as those calculated under the subtraction method for each of the two types of VAT.

The second basic method of computing tax liabilities under the VAT, the addition method, takes a different approach. It recognizes that value added under the income concept equals the sum of factor payments and profits. Thus under the addition method the statutory rate is applied directly to value added, as under the subtraction method. But value added is calculated by adding together factor payments and profits. By its very nature the addition method is suitable only for the implementation of the income type VAT, and only the calculation for that type of tax is shown in Table 4.[19] Liabilities are, of course, the same as under the subtraction and credit methods.

One of the reasons for the popularity of the credit method VAT in Europe is the automatic production of documents that can be used in enforcment of the tax both up and down the line in the productive process. A firm's need to have proof of purchases or of tax payments made on purchases (under the subtraction and tax credit approaches, respectively) creates demands for receipts which provide information to the revenue agents about sales of the firm's suppliers. Or, viewed from the other end, receipts issued by a supplier contain information useful in the validation of the purchasing firm's claims of purchases made or taxes paid.[20] Information gained in this way is also potentially useful in enforcment of income and other taxes. These self-enforcing features may, however, be fairly unimportant in the U.S., where the level of taxpayer compliance is generally agreed to be higher than in Europe.

The administrative appeal of the addition method, which it shares with the subtraction method, is that most of the records it requires are internal to the firm. But whereas the firm's interest in understating sales and overstating purchases is countered by the opposite pressures of its customers and suppliers under the subtraction or tax credit approaches, under the addition method the desires of the firm and

---

[19] Theoretically a consumption type VAT could be implemented under the addition method, but only if profits were reduced by the amount of net investment.

[20] The subtraction method, described as the "accounts method" in National Economic Development Office, *Value Added Tax* (London: Her Majesty's Stationery Office, 1971), pp. 55-56, would be based upon firms' accounts rather than simply upon invoices. But the accounts would probably need to be substantially different from those now kept and firms would be put in an adversary position vis-à-vis their suppliers and customers, unlike the situation under the addition method.

those of the recipients of the factor payments it makes are likely to be in accord. That is, both benefit from the understatement of factor payments, if there is an income tax as well as a VAT. Moreover, there is little secondary benefit in the form of increased knowledge useful in income tax collection in this case.

The addition method is also markedly inferior to the subtraction and credit methods for other reasons to be noted below. This is especially true if American interest were to focus primarily upon the consumption type VAT, which was suggested before as likely. The choice between the subtraction and credit methods is less clear, as is demonstrated below. But on balance the credit method, which is universally used in Europe, seems preferable. It is primarily in terms of a credit method VAT that the discussion of sections 3 to 7 is framed.

D. Differential Rates. Although one of the advantages usually claimed for the VAT is the neutrality inherent in a uniform ad valorem rate, as noted below, there may be occasions in which rate differentials are either desirable or inevitable. Examples of desirable differentials would be final products or certain stages of production chosen for preferential tax treatment. Less desirable but inevitable differentials include cases in which, for political or administrative reasons, certain stages or products cannot easily be subjected to the otherwise general rate of tax and cases in which tax rates are altered temporarily for macroeconomic reasons. The implications of the various methods of calculating the tax under these conditions are spelled out here.

Differentials desired. If it is desired as a matter of social policy to tax certain *final products* at higher or lower rates than the generally prevailing rate, the goal can be achieved conveniently only under the tax credit method. A general and important characteristic of this approach is that only the rate applied at the last stage in the production-distribution process matters, since credit is received by the firm at this stage for all taxes it has paid on purchases. Thus if it were desired to exempt food for equity reasons or to encourage housing construction as a matter of national policy, exemptions from the VAT could be allowed for these items at the final stage. Credits (or refunds) would eliminate any burden imposed by the taxes previously paid on inputs into the exempt product at earlier stages. (Notice that only to the extent that it built houses would the construction industry be favored.)

Under both the subtraction and addition methods the tax rate prevailing at each stage is applied literally to the value added at that stage. Exemption or differential taxation of the final stage would therefore be of little consequence for products with relatively little value added at that stage, unless rebates could be provided for taxes previously incorporated in the prices of inputs. Thus differential taxation of final products would be difficult to achieve, and an unsuccessful attempt to achieve it by taxing only the final stage differentially would favor products, production processes, and firms with relatively large (or small, depending on the differential) fractions of value added occurring at the last stage. In short, differential treatment of final goods requires the tax credit approach.

On the other hand, if a given productive *activity* (for example, agriculture) is to be favored as a matter of public policy, the tax credit approach is conceptually inferior to the other two means of calculating tax liabilities. Precisely because the rate at the last stage is the only one that matters under this approach, the rates levied at previous stages are irrelevant and it is impossible to treat different activities differently.[21]

Conversely, either the addition or subtraction method theoretically provides differential treatment of activities quite easily. As noted above, both methods apply the tax rate for each stage directly to value added at that stage. As a practical matter, however, it would be difficult to apply differential rates to the various outputs of a given multiproduct firm under the subtraction method.[22] Thus the tax credit method allows differential taxation of products, but not of activities, and the other two approaches allow activities, but not products, to be taxed differentially.

---

[21] This is not quite true since credits can be granted for taxes "as if" paid, as has been done in Holland and Ireland; see "VAT in Europe," *The Economist*, March 25, 1972, p. 65. But such schemes are difficult to administer. Note in addition that there is considerable difference between a stage being exempted from the tax on value added and a stage being kept in the VAT system but taxed at a zero rate; the comments in the text apply only in the latter case. Complete exemption from the VAT system would amount to being treated like the household sector and could work a hardship on the firms involved. Thus, suppose that in the example in Table 4 the sales of firms at stage B were exempt from the 10 percent VAT. The stage B firms would pay the tax of $30 on purchases, but being outside the VAT system could claim no credit for those taxes. On the other hand, firms at stage C would pay the full $100 VAT on its sales, but have no credit, since its purchases had not been taxed. The net result of this break in the chain of tax credits is overtaxation equal to the tax paid on sales before the exempt stage, or $30 in this example.

[22] An arbitrary allocation of purchases to sales would be necessary, as it would not be practical to deduct purchases from the sales to which they relate strictly as inputs; see National Economic Development Office, *Value Added Tax*, pp. 15–18, for a short discussion of the points covered in this and the previous footnote.

Differentials not desired. Whereas some products and activities may be the object of consciously differential taxation, others may be taxed differentially solely as a matter of accident or administrative or political necessity, or because macroeconomic conditions require temporary changes in tax rates. By assumption, such differential taxation of products is unintended and undesirable.

Suppose, first, that because of the large number of firms involved it is decided not to extend the VAT to the retail level. The tax would discriminate against industries and processes in which value added occurs early and favor backward integration by retailers (but only if this would not subject the retail price to taxation). But there would be no particular differences in the distortions caused by the three methods of calculating tax liability. Under each approach all value added up to the retail stage would be subject to taxation. Similar comments apply if a particular final product could not be subjected to the VAT for some reason.

If it were some other stage (or activity) at which administrative difficulties or political pressures forced differential rates (or no tax), the situation would be different. Under the addition or subtraction method the value added at the hard-to-tax stage would be taxed relatively lightly, but collections at other stages would not be affected. Thus the favorable treatment of one stage would carry through to the end in the form of a reduced tax burden on goods passing through that stage. On the other hand, under the tax credit approach any difficulties of collection would theoretically be made up in subsequent stages. The differentially lower rates would be reflected in lower credits for taxes paid on purchases. Thus this kind of undesired differential would be more easily overcome if the tax credit approach were employed, so long as at least one taxable stage follows the differentially taxed stage. The more important risk is that complete exemption of one stage from the VAT would result in a break in the chain of credits, so that goods passing through that stage would actually be overtaxed by the amount of taxes collected before the break.[23]

---

[23] See footnote 21 above. A further unintended discrimination may result from variations in tax rates resulting from discretionary manipulation of the VAT rate for stabilization purposes. As suggested previously, under both the addition and subtraction methods the tax rate applied to value added occurring during a given period would be subjected to the tax rate prevailing then. Under the tax credit approach all value added would be subjected to the rate prevailing at the time of final sale. Which approach would be preferable from a stability viewpoint is a largely unexplored question.

E. Border Tax Adjustments. Thus far little has been said of the way value added taxation affects international trade or of border tax adjustments, perhaps (whether rightly or wrongly) the most famous aspect of the administration of the tax. This section examines this important administrative question. How the VAT would affect international trade is the subject of section 4E.

Commodity taxes on products entering international trade can be levied on either of two bases. If the product is taxed where produced, and not where consumed, the tax is an origin-principle tax, or a tax on production. If, on the other hand, the product is taxed where it is consumed, but not where it is produced, we have a destination-principle tax, or a tax on consumption. A retail sales tax is an almost perfect example of a destination-principle tax.[24] Goods (and ideally services) are taxed at their point of sale to ultimate consumers, whether they are produced domestically or imported. Thus the tax is levied only upon consumption, or at the point of destination. On the other hand, a tax on value added levied without border tax adjustments (described below) would be levied on production, or in the nation of origin. For example, referring to Table 1, suppose that the production at stage A took place in one country and that the production at stages B and C took place after importation into another country. Value added on production of $300 occurs in the first country and on production of $700 in the second. Thus each nation could levy its own tax on the production occurring within its borders if it followed the origin principle.[25]

But what if we wished to tax commodities under the VAT where consumed, and only there? In that case we would need to exempt exports from tax and rebate any tax already paid on them, so that they would enter world trade unencumbered by taxes levied in their nation(s) of origin. Similarly, it would be necessary to levy a tax on imports to equalize tax burdens vis-à-vis domestically produced goods. The exemption from, and rebate of, taxes on exports and the com-

---

[24] Conceptually, the retail sales tax is a perfect example. In fact, retail sales taxes are often levied on capital and intermediate goods, and thus included in the price of exports. Moreover, many consumer durables bought in low-tax states by residents of high-tax states to minimize taxes are subjected to the retail sales tax in the state where they are purchased and not to use taxes in the state of residence of the consumers.

[25] Given the virtual certainty that the origin principle would not be considered seriously in the United States, there is no purpose in going into detail in its administration. We might note, however, that it is probably best implemented using the addition or subtraction methods for an income type VAT. An origin-principle tax using the credit method is practically impossible. For a further discussion, see Shoup, *Public Finance*, pp. 262-64.

pensating import duty levied to convert an otherwise origin-principle VAT to a destination-principle are called border tax adjustments (BTA).

An example based upon Table 1 will help to clarify the function and operation of border tax adjustments. Assume as before that stage A occurs in one country and stages B and C occur in another. Then we would want the goods to leave the first country free of tax and to be taxed upon entry into the second, in order that taxation would be based on the country of destination. Tax-free exportation is easily achieved in this one stage example; simply exempting exports from the VAT would suffice. If, however (and contrary to the example), the tax had already been paid at an earlier stage, it would be necessary to rebate it. This is easily achieved under the credit method. The exporter would claim credit for any taxes paid on inputs, including those used to produce exports, against his liability for taxes on domestic sales. (Export sales would be exempt.) Or, if his total credit for taxes paid on inputs exceeded his gross tax liability on domestic sales, he would receive a refund of the credit from the treasury.[26] He would pay the tax on purchases, but be allowed credit or refund for his tax payments, so that on balance exports would occur tax-free. The subtraction method would operate in a similar way. Inputs would be subtracted from domestic sales and the VAT paid on the difference. If that figure were negative, a refund would be due. On the other hand, it would be difficult to administer border tax adjustments under the addition method.

Equalizing the tax burden between imports and domestically produced goods can be achieved simply by taxing the goods at the point of importation, under any of the three methods of calculating tax liabilities. But under the credit method it is not even necessary to tax imports directly, except when they are made by ultimate consumers. So long as the goods pass through at least one taxed transaction after being imported the value added occurring before importation will be taxed. Since there would be no credit for previously paid taxes, the firm making the first taxed sale subsequent to importation would be liable for the tax on the entire value of the goods. In fact, any understatement of value at the time of import would be corrected on subsequent sale under the credit method. Theoretically the same result could be effected under the subtraction

---

[26] All the European countries refund excess credits immediately to the extent that they arise from exports. On the other hand, France applies a "buffer rule" to credits arising from other sources. Under this rule excess credits resulting from investment can only be accumulated and applied to subsequent tax liabilities.

method, but administration would, in reality, probably be much more difficult. Finally, under the addition method any value that was not taxed at import would escape completely, due to the mechanics of the method. Again, the credit method seems administratively superior to the addition and subtraction methods.

It is worth returning briefly to the cascade type turnover tax considered in section 2A above. Suppose that the goods produced in the three industries considered in the example of Table 3 were exported at stage C, instead of being sold to consumers. Ideally the exports would occur tax-free under the destination principle, as noted above. And for industry II tax-free export would be achieved simply by exempting exports from the turnover tax. But for industries in which some value added had occurred at earlier stages, export rebates would be virtually impossible to implement accurately, especially if goods had passed through several stages. This is easily seen by noting that (besides the direct exemption of exports from the tax) rebate of taxes would need to be made at different rates on the value of input purchases in industries I and III. In industry I rebate of $50 of taxes on purchases of $700, or a rate of about 7 percent, would be required, whereas in industry III purchases of $900 would have been taxed a total of $85, or almost 9½ percent. There is no way that rebates could be given automatically and accurately, as under the VAT. Rebates would of necessity be based on averages, which means that discrimination would occur between industries, methods of production, and firms. This is one of the primary disadvantages of the cascade tax.

The situation is, of course, the same on the import side. Ideally, imports would be taxed at the same ad valorem rate as domestic goods at the same stage of production. But we see from Table 3 that by stage C domestic output in the three industries is being taxed in total at rates varying from 5 to 13.5 percent. There is no one rate at which to tax imports.[27]

It is worth repeating at this point that unlike the cascade type turnover tax, the retail sales tax (in its pure form) achieves destination-principle taxation of internationally traded goods automatically.

---

[27] Because of the necessity of using averages, border tax adjustments were not exact under the turnover taxes, as they are under the VAT, and it was generally agreed that Germany, in particular, undercompensated under the old cascade tax. Thus in shifting to the VAT and its perfect equalization, Germany gained a trade advantage, though it was doing something that was perfectly legitimate under the rules of the General Agreement on Tariffs and Trade (GATT). To avoid adverse effects on international monetary stability, Germany initially allowed BTA at only half the rate of the domestic VAT, moving to full BTA at the time of the subsequent revaluation of the mark.

Exports occur tax-free since all sales besides domestic sales to ultimate consumers are exempt. Similarly, imports and domestically produced goods are treated identically since the tax is applied at a given rate to all sales to consumers, regardless of the nation of origin of the taxed commodity. That this is true is especially important since the existence of border tax adjustments under the VAT has drawn so much attention. Those border tax adjustments are necessary solely to provide under the VAT the destination-principle taxation that occurs naturally under the retail sales tax. A VAT with border tax adjustments therefore constitutes no more of a trade advantage than would a retail sales tax since in their pure forms the two taxes are economically equivalent.

F. VAT vs. Retail Sales Tax. Although in theory the VAT and the retail sales tax are economically equivalent, in actuality the two taxes are likely to be different for administrative reasons, quite aside from differences in their tax bases that result from policy decisions. These differences, and the resulting administrative advantages and disadvantages, are reviewed in this section. For the sake of holding the discussion to manageable proportions, the retail sales tax is compared only to the consumption type VAT imposed under the credit method, the most likely candidate for adoption in the United States.[28]

Probably the primary advantage of the value added tax relative to the retail sales tax (RST) involves the treatment of services and capital goods. Under a consumption type VAT, credit is allowed for taxes on all inputs, whether of capital, services, or intermediate goods. Thus only consumer goods and services are taxed under the VAT.[29]

Under the RST the solution is not so simple. Since some goods (and services) can be employed either as productive inputs or as

---

[28] This discussion draws heavily upon Carl S. Shoup, "Experience with Value-Added Tax in Denmark, and Prospects in Sweden," *Finanzarchiv*, March 1969, pp. 236-52 and "Factors Bearing on an Assumed Choice between a Federal Retail Sales Tax and a Federal Value-Added Tax," mimeographed, 1970; and John F. Due, "The Case for Use of the Retail Form of Sales Tax in Preference to the Value Added Tax," mimeographed, 1970. Among minor problems not discussed here are the larger number of firms reached by the VAT, the self-policing features of the VAT, the VAT's unfamiliarity in the U.S., the increased bookkeeping burden on small firms under the VAT, etc. These are all self-explanatory and need only be mentioned here.

[29] There is, of course, a problem of credit taken for taxes on goods purchased for business use but converted to consumption by the owner of the business. This problem seems to be more or less comparable for the two taxes, though under VAT a falsified tax return is required if this result is to be achieved. Shoup has emphasized this point in "Experience with the Value-Added Tax in Denmark."

consumer goods, a way must be found to exempt them from tax when purchased for business use. Otherwise discrimination will occur between domestically produced goods, and accurate border tax adjustments will be impossible because of taxes paid on inputs at earlier stages and incorporated in prices. One approach is to exempt from tax the sales of specific items used largely for business purposes. This is clearly unsatisfactory since for many products this kind of distinction is untenable; steam turbines can be exempted from the tax with little danger of an error in the classification, but hammers and shovels cannot be.[30]

A second approach is to exempt all purchases by registered firms on the assumption that purchases by nonregistered customers will be made almost entirely by consumers. The obvious problem is, of course, guaranteeing both that production inputs are largely free of tax and that not too much otherwise taxable output intended for the private use of the firm's owner passes through tax-exempt transactions. Moreover, businessmen object to the necessity of dividing sales into taxable and exempt categories and accounting for them separately. Authorities differ as to the relative effectiveness of the RST and VAT in handling purchases of business firms, including services and capital goods.[31]

It was noted in section 2D that complete exemption of any stage of the productive process (besides the last) from paying a credit-method VAT on its sales could pose problems. The problem is not that the final output would be undertaxed since the tax would be made up at later stages; it is, rather, that being exempt from tax the firms in the exempt sector might not be allowed credit for taxes paid on their purchases. If the chain of credits were broken, the product would be overtaxed rather than undertaxed. To that extent the VAT would differ from the retail sales tax. This problem may be important, for example, for professional services, which often are outside the VAT system. The importance of this source of double

---

[30] A further problem, not inherent in retail sales taxation, is that in actual practice effort is not usually made to exempt all purchases of business firms from the RST. States adopt rules providing exemption only for goods that are to become "component parts" of final products or that are for "direct use" in the production process. If the retail sales tax is to be a consumption tax, exemption should be allowed for *all* purchases by business firms.

[31] See Shoup, "Choice between Retail Sales Tax and Value-Added Tax," and Due, "Case for Retail Sales Tax." Due notes that it should be possible to implement a hybrid tax that, while essentially a retail sales tax, would allow business firms to buy inputs tax-free, subject to audit, or receive credit for taxes paid on inputs.

taxation depends upon the level of tax rates and the importance of purchased inputs.[32]

Finally, the author has argued at length elsewhere that from the standpoint of intergovernmental relations the federal government should adopt a retail sales tax, rather than a credit type VAT, if it is to adopt either.[33] This contention rests upon the ease of piggy-backing state and local levies on a federal retail sales tax and the difficulty of doing so under a federal VAT.[34] It might be objected that federal use of a retail sales tax would be considered an intrusion into a field of taxation heretofore reserved for the exclusive use of state (and more recently local) governments. But this argument is based more on illusion than on reality, even if the shaky argument that general consumption taxation should be left to the states and localities is granted. Retail sales taxes and value added taxes of the consumption type are basically equivalent, as noted above. Thus a federal retail sales tax would involve no more intrusion into the general consumption tax field than would a VAT.

3. The Tax Base: Practice

The above discussion implies that the VAT would apply at uniform rates to all goods and services. If it did, the tax base, at 1970 income levels, would be $615.8 billion, the total of consumption expenditures in that year (see Table 5). Thus a 3 percent levy would yield almost $20 billion and a 5 percent tax would produce over $30 billion of revenue.

In fact, however, the tax base and revenues are likely to be considerably less than that, for a number of reasons. One of the administratively difficult areas of application of a tax on value added involves owner-occupied housing.[35] Ideally, the VAT would be

---

[32] Shoup has noted in "Experience with the Value-Added Tax in Denmark," p. 243, that professionals may be given the option of entering the VAT system.
[33] Charles E. McLure, Jr., "TVA and Fiscal Federalism," *Proceedings of the 1971 Conference of the National Tax Association*, pp. 279-91. This point is also mentioned by Due, "Case for Retail Sales Tax."
[34] The necessity of a uniform definition of taxable sales in all states would be a distinct plus for such a piggyback approach, provided the federal definition were written with care to achieve accurate taxation of only sales to ultimate consumers. Many state retail sales taxes now impose heavy burdens on business inputs, but exempt services. Moreover, piggybacking would probably eliminate the need for use taxes, one of the most troublesome features of existing state retail sales taxes.
[35] Conceptually there is no similar problem with regard to rental housing, which could be handled like any other business venture. However, small amounts of value added tax would need to be collected from a large number of landlords with no other taxable receipts.

applied to sales of new houses and owner occupants would be charged the tax on the gross value of imputed rental income, as though they were renting the housing to themselves. Correspondingly, owners of houses would be allowed credit for taxes paid on houses at the time of their purchase and on repairs, improvements, etc.[36] On balance, owner-occupied housing would be taxed on a consumption basis like rental housing and other goods and services. But this ideal solution involves the imputation of rental income to owner occupants, a problem that for years has stymied proposals to include this element of income in taxable income. There would seem to be little chance that this approach would be implemented. Thus a deduction from the $615.8 billion potential tax base mentioned above is almost certain.

A compromise solution would be to treat owner-occupied housing as a consumption item, rather than as a capital good, and tax it at the time of purchase, with no subsequent tax credit or imputation of rental income. Taxing owner-occupied housing in this way, and rental housing as any other business, would result in a reduction of the tax base by $41.7 billion to $574.1 billion (see Table 5). Certainly this approach would be administratively feasible, and presumably it would be applied to consumer durables such as automobiles and household appliances. But it would discriminate against owner-occupied housing relative to rental housing and other goods and services, and it would favor present homeowners relative to new homeowners.[37] This discrimination would help to offset the favorable income tax treatment of housing that currently exists, but it is unlikely to be politically acceptable, since a 5 percent VAT would add $1,000 directly to the price of a $20,000 home.[38]

Since owner-occupied housing is not likely to be taxed either immediately as a consumer good or over time by imputation, it might not be taxed at all. If not, then rents on rental residences should not be taxed since to tax them would accentuate the preferential treatment accorded owner-occupied housing under the income tax. Complete exemption of housing would serve to offset the high sales tax

---

[36] Since immediate credit for taxes on house purchases would far exceed gross liabilities for taxes on imputed rental income, carry-over of credits or refunds would be necessary, as is true in other instances of large net investment.

[37] A true consumption type VAT would treat tenants and existing and future homeowners equally, by taxing the imputed rental value of all owner-occupied housing at the same rate that would apply to house rents.

[38] For a recent analysis of the income tax advantages of investment in owner-occupied housing, see Henry Aaron, "Income Taxes and Housing," *American Economic Review*, December 1970, pp. 789-806.

equivalents of existing property taxes, and might accord with social priorities in any case.[39] If housing were removed from the tax base entirely, the latter would fall below total personal consumption expenditures by $91.2 billion, to $524.6 billion, at 1970 income levels.

Next, there are other items of consumption that are intrinsically difficult to tax under any consumption tax. Perhaps the most obvious examples are domestic services and expenditures abroad by Americans. Much more important are the services of financial intermediaries, including insurance companies. The difficulties involved in the taxation of financial institutions can be seen in the following quotation from Shoup:

> *Banks, insurance companies, and other financial institutions are exempt* from the Danish value-added tax simply, it is said, because of the difficulty of applying to them the concepts of total sales and taxable purchases. Interest as such is of course not subject to the consumption-type of value-added tax; but "interest" as a payment for services rendered by a bank free of direct charge (e.g. free check books and checking services) is in principle taxable. Such a service would have to be given an imputed value, and divided into that part rendered to business firms and that part rendered to households, so that the tax levied on the service rendered to firms could be taken by those firms as a credit against the tax on their own sales. An approximate solution would be to tax the financial institution on its payroll, and divide this tax between the two groups of customers on some relevant basis, perhaps number of checks handled, but Denmark has been unwilling to attempt this or any other rough substitute. Meanwhile the exclusion of these financial institutions from the value-added tax system has caused some difficulty. The banks have set up a cooperative electronic data processing institute to perform services for the smaller banks, but these services are held taxable, and the small banks get no tax credit, being themselves exempt. The larger banks perform their own EDP services, and pay no tax on that value added.[40]

---

[39] Dick Netzer in *Economics of the Property Tax* (Washington, D. C.: Brookings Institution, 1966), pp. 29-31, 106, estimates that property taxes now represent the equivalent of about a 20-25 percent sales tax on housing.

[40] Shoup, "Experience with the Value-Added Tax in Denmark," p. 245. It should be noted that a problem exists only for services provided directly to households. The value of services provided to the business sector would be included in their value added under the credit method. In fact in this case the more important problem would be overtaxation because of breaking the chain of tax credits, as noted above.

Deduction of the $38.4 billion involved in these three items, plus a number of minor items, after the complete exemption of housing, would reduce the likely tax base (at 1970 levels) to $486.2 billion (see Table 5).[41]

Third, some items included in the total for personal consumption expenditures are likely to be excluded from the tax base as a matter of social policy. It is almost inconceivable that the tax would be applied to private education and research and to religious and welfare activities. Moreover, medical care expenses, funeral expenses, and perhaps legal expenses could very well also be exempt as a matter of social policy.[42] Deductions for these items, totaling $74.4 billion, would reduce the tax base further to $411.8 billion.

Moreover, several kinds of utilities might be exempt from the tax, especially as they are often provided by municipal governments. In addition, taxing them might be thought to add too much to the regressivity of the tax. Examples would be household utilities and purchased local transportation. Deductions for these items are placed at $26.8 billion, leaving a tax base of $385.0 billion at 1970 income

---

[41] It may be worthwhile to explain the construction of Table 5. The first column simply shows the composition of personal consumption expenditures in 1970. Column 2 provides an illustration of the effect of treating owner-occupied housing as a consumer durable item. Since this treatment is unlikely to materialize, this column is included for comparison only. Column 3 shows the effects of eliminating from the tax base housing and other items that for administrative reasons are hard to tax. From the total of consumption expenditures of $615.8 billion given in column 1 the sum of these items, $129.6 billion, is subtracted, leaving $486.2 billion. In the remainder of the columns exemptions that might be made as a matter of social policy, for utilities, and for food are treated analogously. Each of these potential exemptions is subtracted from a tax base already reduced by the amounts shown in previous columns (except column 2). Thus the $100.5 billion for food in column 6 is subtracted from the tax base of $385.0 billion shown in column 5; the latter figure reflects exemption for housing, "socially justified" exemptions, and exemption for utilities.

[42] Organizations in these fields could be kept in the system, but taxed at a zero rate. Thus they would receive credit for any taxes paid on purchases. Similar treatment could be accorded state and local governments. This approach is far superior to attempting to exempt sales to these organizations and governments from the tax. The assumption that nonprofit organizations, governments, and firms in sectors exempted from the VAT would be granted refunds for taxes paid on all purchases may not be totally realistic, but it appears to be a reasonable working hypothesis for the present analysis. It allows us to employ consumption figures from the national income accounts in estimating the tax base.

In his testimony before the Joint Economic Committee on March 22, 1972, Norman Ture makes the interesting point that the VAT would not truly be a consumption-based tax unless expenditures on investment in human capital, as well as physical capital, were exempt. This provides a strong rationale for the exemption of much of both educational and medical expenses. (One could carry this reasoning to the ridiculous extreme by applying it to the activities of religious organizations—treating them as *really* long-term investment!)

Table 5
PERSONAL CONSUMPTION EXPENDITURES AND ADJUSTMENTS FOR POTENTIAL EXEMPTIONS FROM BASE, 1970 LEVELS
($ in billions)

| Type of Product | Total Personal Consumption (1) | Exclusion of Imputed Rent and Taxation of Purchase Price of Owner-occupied Homes[a] (2) | Adjustments for Housing Exemption and Other Administrative Exemptions[a] | | | |
| | | | Adjustment for Socially Justified Exemptions | | Adjustment for Exemption of Utilities, etc. | |
			With no other adjustments (3)	No other adjustments (4)	No other adjustments (5)	Adjustment for food (6)
Food and tobacco	$142.9	—	−2.8[b]	—	—	−100.5[l]
Clothing, accessories, and jewelry	62.3	—	−0.2[c]	—	—	—
Personal care	10.1	—	—	—	—	—
Housing	91.2	−41.7	−91.2	—	—	—
Household operations	85.6	—	−4.7[d]	—	−23.7[i]	—
Medical care expenses	47.3	—	—	−47.3	—	—
Personal business	35.5	—	−23.2[e]	−6.0[g]	—	—
Transportation	77.9	—	—	—	−2.1[j]	—
Recreation	39.0	—	—	−1.9[h]	−1.0[k]	—
Public education and research	10.4	—	—	−10.4	—	—

Religious and welfare activities	8.8	—	—	−8.8	—	—
Foreign travel and other, net	4.8	—	−7.5[f]	—	—	—
Total	615.8	−41.7	−129.6	−74.4	−26.8	−100.5
Previously detailed adjustments	—	—	—	−129.6	−204.0	−230.8
Total adjustments	—	−41.7	−129.6	−204.0	−230.8	−331.3
Tax base after adjustments	—	574.1	486.2	411.8	385.0	284.5
Tax base as percent of total personal consumption expenditures	—	93.2%	79.0%	66.9%	62.5%	46.2%

a Treatment of housing as consumption expenditure included for comparison only. Further calculations assume complete exemption of housing.

b Food furnished government and military employees and food produced and consumed on farms.

c Standard clothing issued to military personnel.

d Domestic service.

e Services furnished without payment by financial institutions, including expense of handling life insurance.

f Foreign travel by U.S. residents and expenditures abroad by U.S. government personnel.

g Legal services and funeral and burial expenses.

h Legitimate theaters and opera, and entertainments of nonprofit institutions; clubs and fraternal organizations except insurance.

i Household utilities (except telephone and telegraph).

j Bridge, tunnel, ferry and road tolls; street and electric railway and local bus.

k Pari-mutuel net receipts.

l Food purchased for off-premise consumption.

Source: Derived from U.S. Department of Commerce, *Survey of Current Business*, July 1971, part 1, tables 2.5 and 7.3.

levels. Finally, the $100.5 billion worth of food purchased for off-premise consumption might very well be exempted, also in an effort to reduce the regressivity of the tax.[43] In such a case the tax base would be but $284.5 billion, or 46 percent of personal consumption expenditures.

Table 5 indicates the size of the tax base under various combinations of exemptions. It is almost certain that in practice the base (at 1970 levels of consumption) would not be much larger than $500 billion, and it might be as small as $300 billion. In the former case a 3 percent tax would yield $15 billion and a 5 percent tax $25 billion. But in the latter case those two rates would provide revenue of only $9 billion and $15 billion. To place these estimates in perspective, we can note that in 1970 the corporation income tax yielded $32.8 billion (national income accounts basis).

4. Economic Effects

In this section we examine the economic effects of substituting a consumption type tax on value added for part of the corporation income tax. In particular, we discuss how this tax substitution would affect the neutrality of the tax system, the rates of saving, investment, and economic growth, the success of efforts to use tax policy to stabilize the economy, and the nation's balance of payments. Effects upon the distribution of income are considered in the next section.

One might reasonably ask why cast the entire discussion of this study in terms of substituting VAT for part of the corporation income tax (or other taxes), especially when the VAT could be considered as a new source of additional revenue. The answer is simple. Most obviously, virtually the entire discussion of VAT up to now has been precisely in terms of a replacement for part of the corporation income tax. But more important, the VAT cannot be considered in a vacuum, even if it is considered as a new source of revenue. There is almost always an alternative tax that could be used instead of the VAT as a source of additional revenue.[44] Thus it makes sense to compare the

---

[43] It is argued below that a superior approach to the alleviation of regressive taxation would be the allowance of refundable credits against personal income taxes of a given amount of value added taxes or a general program of low-income relief. The estimate presented here is made only for completeness, as there is a good chance that food would be exempted.

[44] Of course we might also consider forgoing the added expenditure, financing it through inflation, or using tight monetary policy to choke off enough private spending to prevent inflation in the face of increased federal outlays. Comparison of VAT with these alternatives would take us far beyond the scope of this study.

VAT with alternative taxes that could be imposed or raised. One such alternative form of increased federal financing is an increase in the corporation income tax. Other obvious alternatives, increases in the payroll and personal income taxes, are considered briefly in section 6 below. The possibility of using revenues from a federal tax on value added to replace revenues from the local school property tax is considered even more summarily in section 7. A federal retail sales tax would, of course, have about the same economic and distributional effects as a VAT.

A. Digression on Incidence. Almost any careful discussion of substituting a value added tax for the corporation income tax quickly digresses into a discussion of the incidence of the two taxes, since virtually all of the effects of the substitution depend crucially upon that question.[45] (Most obviously, the distributional implications of such a tax substitution depend directly upon the incidence of the taxes, that is, upon who bears their burdens.) Thus in this section we digress momentarily at the beginning of our discussion of the economic and distributional effects of substituting a VAT for part of the corporation income tax (CIT) to consider explicitly the incidence of the two taxes. We cannot hope to settle the issue, but we can lay out the arguments. Then in what follows we can simply describe the implications of the tax substitution under various incidence assumptions, leaving to the reader the choice of the most relevant set of assumptions and implications. Those familiar with the literature on tax incidence can, of course, proceed directly to section 4B.

A consumption type VAT would almost certainly be borne by households roughly in proportion to consumption expenditures, though this view is not universally held.[46] Thus primary interest in

---

[45] For the purpose of the present discussion it is sufficient to think of tax incidence as a matter of how a given tax affects relative prices and of who bears the burden of the tax because of induced price changes. A conceptually "clean" definition of incidence would take us further afield than is justified. For further details on the methodology of incidence analysis, see Charles E. McLure, Jr., "Tax Incidence, Absolute Prices, and Macroeconomic Policy," *Quarterly Journal of Economics*, May 1970, pp. 254-67 and "The Theory of Tax Incidence with Imperfect Factor Mobility," *Finanzarchiv*, 1971, pp. 27-48.

[46] For a convincing argument to this effect, see Richard A. Musgrave, *Theory of Public Finance* (New York: McGraw-Hill Book Co., 1959), chapter 16. For two contrary views, see John F. Due, "Sales Taxes and the Consumer," *American Economic Review*, December 1963, pp. 1078-84, and the testimony by Norman Ture before the Joint Economic Committee on March 22, 1972 and Ture's essay in this volume.

this discussion focuses not upon the incidence of the VAT, but upon the incidence of the corporation income tax, which is far less certain.

Traditional theory holds that any tax on economic profits can only be borne by recipients of profit income, at least in the short run. According to that theory, prices in competitive industries equal the marginal costs of marginal firms that, having no profits, pay no tax. On the other hand, a firm that has a monopoly position in an industry maximizes profits by setting marginal costs equal to marginal revenue. In either case the existence of the profits tax, which affects neither marginal costs nor marginal revenue, has no effect on the determination of price. Thus, the reasoning goes, the tax is reflected in lower profits net of tax.[47]

But there is a multitude of reasons for believing that the corporation income tax is (at least partly) shifted, either to consumers or to labor.[48] First, corporate income for tax purposes includes the return to equity capital, and is not comprised solely of economic profits. Thus part of the tax does constitute an element of costs. Second, important portions of the corporate sector of the U.S. economy fit neither the perfect competition nor the pure monopoly mold, and oligopoly behavior is quite consistent with substantial shifting of the corporation tax. The tax, for example, may act as a signal for firms setting prices in a consciously parallel fashion, whether with or without an established price leader. Moreover, wage settlements with strong unions may result in labor sharing the burden of such a tax. Finally, corporate goals other than short-run profit maximization (e.g. avoidance of antitrust action, constrained sales maximization, or limit-pricing based on long-range profit maximization) may lead to shifting of the tax. Thus one can find strong theoretical support on both sides of the incidence argument.[49]

Unfortunately, empirical work done on this subject over the past decade leaves us very much in the dark. The pioneering work by Krzyzaniak and Musgrave found that the tax is completely shifted in manufacturing, a result not theoretically inconsistent with the oligop-

---

[47] Arnold C. Harberger has argued in "The Incidence of the Corporation Income Tax," *Journal of Political Economy*, June 1962, pp. 215-40, that the tax is borne by all recipients of capital income rather than only owners of corporate shares. This qualification is ignored in this discussion; however, it would not seriously alter any of the conclusions.

[48] For a summary of both the traditional theory and most of the important qualifications to it, see Musgrave, *Theory of Public Finance*, chapter 13.

[49] It is worth noting that businessmen seem almost universally to take for granted that the tax is shifted.

oly structure of much of manufacturing.[50] But this analysis has been subjected to considerable criticism, and it seems best to report only that the jury is still out on the question of the short-run incidence of the corporation income tax.[51]

Finally, it is not even clear whether the short- or long-run incidence of the tax is of more importance for policy purposes. For questions of economic neutrality, economic growth, stabilization policy, and the balance of payments, short-run effects are crucial. But where equity is concerned, it may be more useful to consider the incidence in a long-run context.[52]

Given the uncertainty about the answers to important questions of the incidence of the corporation income tax, it seems best, as noted above, to present the arguments of this and the next section under alternative assumptions. Even then, however, only two extreme views are considered—that the tax is borne by recipients of capital income and that it is shifted to consumers. Neither intermediate positions, such as 50 percent shifting, nor alternative shifting assumptions, such as partial shifting to labor, are considered. Intermediate shifting assumptions lead to intermediate results and need not be considered explicitly. Shifting to labor, while theoretically possible, does not have widespread professional support, and the added complication of including it in the analysis does not seem justified.

B. Allocational Efficiency (Neutrality). One of the chief advantages of the VAT, at least in its ideal form, is its allocational neutrality. Because the tax ideally would apply at equal rates to all goods and services (consumption variety) or to all factors incomes (income

---

[50] Marian Krzyzaniak and Richard A. Musgrave, *The Shifting of the Corporation Income Tax* (Baltimore: Johns Hopkins Press, 1963). It should be noted that this study offers no conclusions as to the methods or direction of shifting.

[51] Among the best critiques of the work by Krzyzaniak and Musgrave are Richard E. Slitor, "Corporate Tax Incidence: Economic Adjustments to Differentials under a Two-Tier Tax Structure," and Richard Goode, "Rates of Return, Income Shares, and Corporate Tax Incidence," both in Marian Krzyzaniak, ed., *Effects of Corporation Income Tax* (Detroit: Wayne State University Press, 1966), pp. 136-206 and pp. 207-46, respectively; Robert J. Gordon, "The Incidence of the Corporation Income Tax in U.S. Manufacturing, 1925-62," *American Economic Review*, September 1967, pp. 731-58; and John G. Cragg, Arnold C. Harberger, and Peter Mieszkowski, "Empirical Evidence on the Incidence of the Corporation Income Tax," *Journal of Political Economy*, December 1967, pp. 811-21. Replies and rejoinders appear in Krzyzaniak, ed., *Effects of Corporation Income Tax*, pp. 247-61, *American Economic Review*, December 1968, pp. 1358-67, and *Journal of Political Economy*, July-August, 1970, pp. 768-77.

[52] For a penetrating analysis of the proper time frame for the question of tax incidence and distributional equity, see Marian Krzyzaniak, "Differential Incidence of Taxes on Profits and on Factor Incomes," *Finanzarchiv*, 1971, pp. 464-88.

variety), it would distort no decision as to the way consumers spend their incomes or the way goods and services are produced.[53]

This neutrality may be difficult to comprehend in the abstract, but nonneutrality is easily understood when we examine the corporation income tax, even if we ignore the tax preferences in the existing law. Assume for the moment that the corporation income tax is not shifted. In such a case it discriminates against equity financing and in favor of loan finance. Moreover, since the tax is collected only on corporations, it creates a long-run tendency for underutilization of the corporate form of business organization.[54] And since some products can realistically be produced only if the corporate form is used, the tax also discriminates between products. Finally, since the tax is levied only on one type of return to capital, and not on labor, it discourages use of capital-intensive methods of production in the corporate sector. In the long run, capital investment is likely to be misallocated toward the products of the noncorporate sector. Thus the corporation income tax is distinctly nonneutral.[55]

This observation is true even if the tax is shifted to consumers or to workers. If it is shifted to consumers, it is a capricious sales tax on the products of the corporate sector, and diverts consumption choices away from those products.[56] If it is shifted to workers, it also discriminates in the long run against production in the corporate sector.

---

[53] It should be noted that in the strict sense only the consumption type VAT is truly neutral because the income type VAT taxes saving and therefore is not neutral between present and future consumption; see Musgrave, *Theory of Public Finance*, pp. 374-82. This distortion is ignored here, though it is discussed in a different context in sections 6A and 6B.

[54] This effect may, of course, be offset by the congruence of high-marginal tax rates and preferential treatment of long-term capital gains under the personal income tax.

[55] For an attempt to measure the welfare cost resulting from the nonneutrality of a non-shifted corporation income tax, see Arnold C. Harberger, "Efficiency Effects of Taxes on Income from Capital," in Krzyzaniak, ed., *Effects of Corporation Income Tax*, pp. 107-117. Harberger takes account of existing tax preferences in his analysis. A further waste that is difficult to quantify is the excessive expenses incurred in the corporate sector because the federal government shares in all costs as well as all profits.

[56] This nonneutrality is not solely in terms of *final* products of the corporate sector. The distortion occurs to the extent that the value added in the final product passes through the corporate sector. For an attempt to quantify the distortions introduced by the corporation tax by using input-output analysis to take account of the tax reflected in higher input prices, see Henry Aaron, "The Differential Price Effects of a Value-Added Tax," *National Tax Journal*, June 1968, pp. 162-75. This analysis suffers, as Aaron recognizes, from the use of a value added tax of the gross product type, rather than a VAT of the income or consumption variety.

Not surprisingly, the neutrality of the ideal value added tax is one of the strongest arguments in favor of substituting the VAT for part of the notoriously nonneutral corporation income tax.

However, comparing the conceptually pure VAT with the existing corporation income tax is hardly fair or instructive. As was noted in section 3, it is almost certain that any VAT that might be adopted will not apply at uniform rates to all consumption expenditures. Because they are difficult to tax, housing, the services of financial institutions, and household services will almost certainly be treated differently from all other uses of income. Moreover, items such as food, medical care, funeral and legal services, and utilities might be exempted from the tax as a matter of social policy or to prevent it from being overly regressive. Finally, preferential treatment will be accorded to any industry or pressure group politically potent enough to achieve it. The net result is likely to be a combination of tax base and rate structure that differs considerably from the ideal tax applied at a uniform rate to all value added. Estimates in Table 5 suggest that from one-fifth to over half of personal consumption might be excluded from the tax base. Thus it is far from clear that the VAT would, in practice, be much more neutral from an allocative standpoint than the corporation income tax.[57] This consideration suggests that exemptions for administrative reasons and exemptions intended to reduce the regressivity of the VAT should be kept to a minimum, especially since there are other more nearly neutral ways of reducing regressivity at the lower end of the income scale.

Finally, it should be noted that while substituting a VAT for part of the corporation income tax would eliminate the distortions inherent in the latter, it would do so only at the expense of creating an

---

[57] One potential basis for optimism is the possibility that demand for the items likely to be tax-exempt is relatively insensitive to price. If it is, the tax would not seriously distort consumer choices, even though it drove a nonuniform wedge between marginal costs of production and market prices. This is, of course, an empirical question. But it seems unlikely that demand would be price inelastic for as much as 20-50 percent of the entire market basket of consumers. This is especially true where housing and food are concerned. The quantity of housing and food consumption, whatever that may mean, may be more or less invariant to price, but the quality of housing and food consumed almost certainly is not. Thus exemption of these items would probably result in a greater shift toward expenditures on them than would occur under a truly general tax on value added or retail sales tax. Of course if housing were exempted as a matter of public policy, rather than simply for administrative reasons, we could not consistently term the resulting shift to higher housing expenditure the result of price distortion. Presumably the shift would be the objective of the exemption. Only if exemption results solely from administrative difficulties of taxing some items or efforts to lessen regressivity, rather than from a deliberate public policy decision to favor certain activities, can we legitimately say that it distorts choices.

important new distortion. To the extent that the corporation income tax were eliminated, corporate profits would be taxed only if distributed to shareholders. Thus there would be substantial pressures to retain a greater proportion of earnings and thereby convert profits taxable under the personal income tax as ordinary income, if distributed, into preferentially taxed long-term capital gains. This result would have important consequences for the rate of private saving, the incidence of the tax system, and income distribution. But of more relevance to the immediate discussion, it would constitute a substantial nonneutrality in favor of existing high-profit industries and firms and against low-profit and new undertakings. Firms with substantial profits would not need to stand the test of the marketplace in competing for funds. Double taxation of dividends, itself nonneutral, would have been traded for a substantial tax shelter in retained earnings. This result could be avoided most directly by integrating the corporate and personal income taxes, and less directly by increasing the taxation of long-term capital gains. Many opponents, and even some advocates of the VAT, argue that some such measure should accompany partial substitution of a VAT for the corporation income tax.[58]

C. Growth. One point usually made in favor of a consumption type VAT is that it would be more favorable to saving and economic growth than many of the present components of our tax system. Moreover, the argument goes, elimination of the corporation income tax would reduce the penalty this tax now imposes upon innovation, efficiency, and profitability, and thereby encourage investment and economic growth. In examining the validity of these contentions it will be convenient to address separately the two sides of the saving-investment question. It will be assumed in this section, of course, that the corporation tax is not shifted; if the tax were shifted, the tax substitution would have little effect on either saving or investment.

Private saving. There is little doubt that substitution of the VAT for part of an unshifted corporation income tax would increase savings.

---

[58] Integration of the two income taxes involves treating corporate profits as though they were earned by a partnership and allocating them to shareholders, to be included in the individual income tax returns of the latter, rather than imposing a separate income tax on corporations. Thus corporate profits would be taxed to the individual at his own marginal tax rate, whether distributed or retained. For the arguments for and against integration, see Musgrave, *Theory of Public Finance*, pp. 173-75 and Richard Goode, *The Corporation Income Tax* (New York: John Wiley and Sons, 1951). For examples of how complete and partial integration would work, see Joseph A. Pechman, *Federal Tax Policy*, rev. ed. (Washington, D. C.: Brookings Institution, 1971), pp. 140-47.

Approximately five-sixths of increases in net corporate profits flow into retained earnings.[59] Thus a reduction of, say, $10 billion in the corporation income tax would be reflected in an increase in retained earnings of over $8 billion, which would be supplemented by saving out of the increased dividends made possible by the tax reduction. To be offset against this sum would be a reduction in personal saving of something like $500 million resulting from imposition of the VAT. Thus on balance it would appear that an increase in total private saving of roughly $8 billion would be induced by the $10 billion tax substitution.[60]

Federal budget surplus. It is usual to think explicitly of how structural tax policy affects the level of private saving, but much less frequent to ask about the role of tax policy in determining the amount of saving achieved through the federal budget. Since total saving comprises both private saving and the public surplus, it is well to consider both components in our discussion.

Whereas the level of private saving is influenced largely by the *structure* of taxes, the amount of saving effected through budget policy (assuming a given amount of expenditures) depends primarily upon the *level* of taxes. Since in principle the level, as well as the structure, of taxation is a matter for policy determination, we have more latitude in setting fiscal policies to increase the nation's saving rate than merely adjusting the structure of the tax system, say by substituting VAT for part of the corporation income tax. We should be able to increase total saving by increasing taxes and the budget surplus, as well as by using structural tax policy to induce more private saving (assuming the maintenance of full employment).[61]

---

[59] William H. Oakland, "Automatic Stabilization and the Value-Added Tax," in Albert Ando, E. Cary Brown, and Ann F. Friedlaender, eds., *Studies in Economic Stabilization* (Washington, D. C.: Brookings Institution, 1965), pp. 41-60. Oakland's estimate comes from John Lintner, "Distribution of Incomes of Corporations Among Dividends, Retained Earnings, and Taxes," *American Economic Review*, May 1956, pp. 97-113 and John Brittain, "The Tax Structure and Corporate Dividend Policy," *American Economic Review*, May 1964, pp. 272-87.

[60] This estimate ignores the (slight) possibility that stockholders would reduce personal saving because of the increase in their personal wealth resulting from the increase in retained earnings. Moreover, no account is taken of the increased capital gains tax liabilities that would be paid on the higher stock prices due to increased corporate retention of earnings. Finally, it is worth noting that a considerable amount of this increased flow of retained equity capital would be locked in by the desire to avoid capital gains taxes. This probable result emphasizes the need to tighten the taxation of capital gains if VAT is to replace the corporation income tax.

[61] For an excellent statement of this proposition, see Richard A. Musgrave, "Growth with Equity," *American Economic Review*, May 1963, pp. 323-33.

Investment. It seems intuitively clear at first glance that reduction of the corporation income tax would result in more innovation and investment since the tax penalizes success in risk-taking. If this is true, then substitution of the VAT for the corporation tax would increase investment since the VAT is essentially neutral with regard to risk-taking and investment.

However, this view neglects the obverse side of the penalty on success represented by the federal sharing of gains from productive investment. By the same token that the federal government, via the corporation income tax, shares in profits from successful ventures, it assumes part of losses incurred in unsuccessful ventures, so long as adequate allowance is made for offsetting losses against gains from other undertakings or profits realized in other periods. Thus it is not clear on theoretical grounds whether on balance the corporation income tax should be expected to discourage investment and innovation or to encourage them. Theoretical analysis based upon notions of utility maximization and portfolio selection suggests, however, that for a given stock of funds encouragement of risk-taking may be the more likely outcome.[62] If so, investment out of a given flow of corporate saving is likely to be somewhat less under the VAT than under the corporation income tax, contrary to our original intuitive notion. Nonetheless, the far more important factor may be the much larger amounts of retained earnings likely to be generated under the VAT.

This conclusion is suggested strongly by empirical analysis linking investment to the cash flow of corporations. According to one set of estimates, as much as 80-90 percent of the increase in cash flow would eventually find its way directly into increased investment.[63] Thus an increase of as much as $8-9 billion might result from a $10 billion VAT-corporation tax substitution. Though the determinants of investment are the subject of considerable debate, and the effect might not be this great, it seems safe to predict a marked rise in investment. However, and this is worth repeating, such would be the case only if the existing corporation income tax is not shifted.

---

[62] The path-breaking analysis of this problem was by Evsey D. Domar and Richard A. Musgrave, "Proportional Income Taxation and Risk-taking," *Quarterly Journal of Economics*, May 1944, pp. 387-422. It has been given increasing rigor and sophistication in James Tobin, "Liquidity Preference as Behavior Towards Risk," *Review of Economic Studies*, February 1958, pp. 65-87 and Joseph E. Stiglitz, "The Effects of Income, Wealth, and Capital Gains Taxation on Risk Taking," *Quarterly Journal of Economics*, May 1969, pp. 263-83.

[63] See Charles W. Bischoff, "Business Investment in the 1970s: A Comparison of Models," *Brookings Papers on Economic Activity*, 1971(1), pp. 13-58, especially p. 47.

Summary. Substitution of VAT for part of the corporation income tax would increase private savings substantially—perhaps by as much as 80 percent of the amount of the tax change—if the latter tax is not shifted. (If the corporation tax is shifted, little change would result from the tax substitution.) Thus, it should be conducive to a higher rate of economic growth, provided the added saving flows into investment rather than simply acting as a drag on the economy and causing unemployment. The actual outcome depends itself upon budget policy. It seems reasonable to assume, however, that the bulk of the increased cash flow resulting from the tax substitution would flow into investment, raising the efficiency and the rate of growth of the economy.

Of course, budget policy plays a role on both sides of the saving-investment equation. Private saving can be supplemented by an increased budget surplus (or reduced deficit). It might appear that saving from this source would be largely sterile if corporations prefer strongly to invest internal funds rather than to go to capital markets. But budget surpluses and debt reduction could supply funds for residential construction. The nature of the government tax and monetary policies necessary to assure that result deserves further research, but to pursue the question further here would take us too far afield. Rather, we turn now to a more general discussion of the role of the value added and corporation income taxes in economic stabilization.

D. Stabilization. The impact of the hypothesized tax substitution upon efforts to stabilize the economy along a target path of full employment and price stability can be discussed under three subtopics: the initial effect upon the price level, the relative effectiveness of the VAT and the corporation income tax as automatic stabilizers, and the usefulness of variations in the rates of the two taxes as instruments of discretionary fiscal policy.

Initial effect on prices. Prices would probably rise by the amount of the VAT upon its substitution for the corporation income tax.[64] Under traditional shifting assumptions this is surely so; the VAT would raise prices, but the lowering of corporate tax rates would not result in offsetting reductions in prices. Only if, contrary to traditional assumptions, the corporate tax is shifted, would we expect the

---

[64] It is, of course, conceivable that the substitution could result in prices rising by even more than the percentage amount of the value added tax. This would be especially true if the initial price increase resulting from the substitution were to induce wage increases via escalator clauses in collective bargaining agreements. The likely extent of this potential phenomenon is unknown.

substitution not to result in higher prices; one shifted tax would replace another. But even if the corporation tax is shifted, it might not be automatically "unshifted" when reduced.[65] If not, higher prices would almost certainly result from the tax substitution. And even if unshifting in the sense of realignment of relative prices were to occur, it might be in the context of a general rise in prices. Thus it seems reasonable to believe that the tax substitution would result in a rise in the price level.[66]

Automatic stability. The effectiveness of various taxes as automatic stabilizers depends upon how tax revenues respond to cyclical variations in the value of national output and the effects that changes in revenues have upon private demand. Corporate profits, and therefore corporation income tax collections, respond strongly to changes in GNP. On the other hand, consumption fluctuates less than GNP, and so would receipts under a consumption type VAT yielding an equal amount of revenue at full employment.

This result is not enough, however, to guarantee that the corporation income tax would be the more effective built-in stabilizer. If the tax is borne out of profits, its increase during the upswing would restrain the net flow of internal funds and would probably hold back investment.[67] But investment might not respond with equal strength to reduced tax collections in the downswing because of the perception of inadequate investment opportunities. If not, the reduced VAT burden on consumers might be the better stimulus to private spending. Thus it is possible that the corporate tax might be more useful in automatically restraining demand in an upswing, but not much more useful than the VAT in cushioning a fall in demand. Of course, if the corporation tax is shifted, the more volatile corporate tax should be the better stabilizer.[68]

---

[65] It is worth noting that the pioneering work by Krzyzaniak and Musgrave that reports complete shifting also finds less than complete unshifting when the tax is removed; *Shifting of the Corporation Income Tax*, p. 58.

[66] The German experience of little rise in prices is not directly applicable here. In Germany a cascade type turnover tax was replaced, whereas the present discussion concerns replacing part of the corporation income tax. The German precedent would be instructive primarily if forward shifting and unshifting of the corporation income tax were assumed. It is also worth noting that the German substitution was preceded by a massive educational campaign aimed at forestalling price increases.

[67] In making statements of this kind it is necessary to assume that monetary policy and the level of autonomous expenditures would be the same in either case (except as fluctuations in tax receipts took money from the private sector).

[68] A menacing possibility is that a shifted corporation tax might raise prices during an upswing to a level that would not fall in a downswing. Presumably a flat-rate VAT would not have this effect.

Discretionary fiscal policy. There seems to be no reason to prefer either the VAT or the corporation income tax as tools of discretionary fiscal policy on the basis of administrative convenience.[69] Both could be changed quickly and easily. However, both theoretical analysis and empirical evidence from the 1968 surcharge suggest that temporary changes in the VAT would be more effective stabilizers than temporary changes in the corporation income tax of similar size. If corporate investment is based on long-range projections of profitability, it is unlikely to be affected much by temporary changes in corporate tax rates.[70] Moreover, if investment behavior is of the accelerator type, the most effective way to influence this behavior might be through consumer purchases. Only if investment is a fairly simple function of contemporaneous flows of internal funds, is it likely to respond strongly to temporary variations in the corporation income tax rate.

On the other hand, consumption might be affected quite strongly by a temporary change in the VAT rate. Not only would much of the tax be collected from persons with high marginal propensities to spend; perhaps more important, variations in the VAT rate, if known to be temporary, would induce postponement or acceleration of purchases, especially of durables. No similar intertemporal substitution effect characterizes changes in the corporation income tax.[71] Thus it seems that the VAT would rank ahead of the corporation income tax as an instrument of discretionary fiscal policy, if the corporation tax is not shifted. Of course, if instantaneous shifting of the corporation tax occurs, variations in that tax supposedly would be as effective in stabilizing output as would changes in the VAT. It is doubtful, however, that the shifting response is so perfect.

Summary. Substitution of the VAT for part of the (unshifted) corporation income tax would probably raise prices by about the

---

[69] It should be noted, however, that executive authority to change tax rates for countercyclical reasons within predetermined limits and subject to congressional veto, while desirable for the corporation income tax, would be essential for the VAT. Otherwise anticipatory buying and postponement of purchases of durables during the discussion of rate changes would perversely affect efforts to stabilize the economy.

[70] Robert Eisner, "Fiscal and Monetary Policy Reconsidered," *American Economic Review*, December 1969, pp. 897-905 and "What Went Wrong," *Journal of Political Economy*, May-June 1971, pp. 629-41. For four comments plus a reply by Eisner, see *American Economic Review*, June 1971, pp. 444-61.

[71] The nearest equivalent under the corporation income tax is the variation in the investment tax credit for stabilization purposes since 1966. Being a tax credit based on the spending of funds, it can have strong intertemporal substitution effects.

amount of the tax. But once enacted, the VAT would probably be a more useful tool of discretionary fiscal policy. On the other hand, the corporation income tax would probably be the more effective built-in stabilizer, especially in the upswing.

E.   **International Aspects.** The value added tax first drew significant attention in the United States when it was recognized that border tax adjustments are allowed under the VAT for products entering international trade. If was felt in some quarters that U.S. reliance on the corporation income tax, for which no border tax adjustments are allowed, together with European conversion to value added taxes, placed American producers at a competitive disadvantage in international markets and was therefore deleterious to the U.S. balance of payments.[72] Moreover, the argument went, the United States could improve its balance of payments by substituting a value added tax for part of the corporation income tax.

There are several separate points in this line of argument that are often confused. First, there is a substantial difference between arguing that the U.S. balance-of-payments position could be improved by substituting a VAT for part of the corporation income tax and arguing that U.S. reliance upon the corporate income tax is in some way disadvantageous to U.S. producers in world markets. The validity of the first contention, which is discussed in detail in the paragraph immediately following, depends upon how the imposition of the VAT and the removal of the CIT would affect prices of internationally traded goods. What the second contention involves is not always made clear, but in most statements favoring the VAT it seems to be assumed that the two arguments are essentially equivalent. To the author this seems to be erroneous. He has argued elsewhere that since the relative reliance of European countries and the U.S. upon direct and indirect taxes has not changed appreciably in the implied direction since the early 1950s, it is more sensible to look to inappropriate exchange rates and differential rates of inflation in the various coun-

---

[72] Among the strong statements of this proposition are Richard W. Lindholm, "National Tax Systems and International Balance of Payments," and Milton Leontiades, "The Logic of Border Taxes," *National Tax Journal*, June 1966, pp. 163-72 and 173-83, respectively.

We have discussed in section 2E the implementation of border tax adjustments for a tax on value added and the way BTA converts an origin-principle tax into a destination-principle tax. The important point in the present context is that under the General Agreement on Tariffs and Trade (GATT) border tax adjustments are allowed for indirect taxes, but not for direct taxes. Thus the corporation income tax, being considered a direct tax, cannot be rebated on exports or levied on imports, as can the VAT, an indirect tax.

tries as the cause of imbalance in the international payments position of the U.S. than to blame that imbalance upon the relative tax structures in the U.S. and its trading partners. [73] This position implies, of course, that the December 1971 realignment of exchange rates should tend to silence complaints about the unfair tax treatment of U.S. firms relative to those in other nations, though in fact it is unlikely to do so.

Turning now to the question of whether or not substituting a VAT for part of the corporation income tax would improve the U.S. balance of payments, several points must be made. First, and most fundamentally, the recent changes in exchange rates should, at least in principle, make the entire discussion—which was germane when the question first arose—*passé*. Since the U.S. was running chronic balance-of-payments deficits in defense of an unrealistic exchange rate, alternatives to devaluation that would improve the balance of trade, and hence the balance of payments, were worth considering. But since exchange rates have been realigned, trying to use tax policy to improve the trade balance still further makes little sense, provided the new exchange rates are equilibrium rates. Only if the dollar is still overvalued and could not be devalued further, might it make sense to try to achieve through tax policy the trade-equilibrating effects of a greater devaluation. But then the overvalued exchange rate, and not the tax structure, should be identified as the culprit in the piece.

Second, whether the tax substitution would in fact improve the balance of trade depends upon how it would affect domestic prices.[74] According to classical incidence assumptions, the VAT (with its compensating import levy) would be reflected in higher prices for all goods in U.S. markets, including imports, but would be rebated on exports, and therefore would leave the general price of exports unchanged. On the other hand, the traditional assumption is that in the short run

---

[73] Charles E. McLure, Jr., "Taxes and the Balance of Payments: Another Alternative Analysis," *National Tax Journal*, March 1968, pp. 57-69. It is noted there that there may be some truth to the contention that U.S. taxation under the corporation income tax is less neutral than European taxation under the VAT, and that this nonneutrality may be worth worrying about. But neutrality is not the stuff that arguments about balance-of-payments positions are made of, and it certainly is not what most advocates of the VAT seem to have had in mind in their discussion of the international aspects of the proposed tax substitution.

[74] This point is similar, but not strictly equivalent, to the question of whether the two taxes are shifted. Tax incidence and shifting depend upon effects upon *relative* prices, while the question at hand is a matter of the effects on absolute prices and price *levels*. Since as a practical matter shifting and unshifting can be expected to occur through changes in absolute prices of taxed products, this distinction is ignored in the text. For more detailed discussions of the issue, see Musgrave, *Theory of Public Finance*, chapter 15 and McLure, "Tax Incidence, Macroeconomic Policy, and Absolute Prices."

the corporation income tax is borne by shareholders, and that its removal would have no impact upon prices. Thus the tax substitution would increase the prices of both imports and U.S. goods by the amount of the tax, and therefore would have no effect upon imports. Similar results apply on the export side. The prices of U.S. exports would be unaffected by the tax substitution, so that no trade improvement would result.

Thus the argument that the tax substitution would improve the U.S. balance of trade involves challenging traditional incidence theory. If, contrary to the traditional assumptions, the corporation income tax is shifted to consumers, removing part of it would lower the prices of U.S. products, provided that the tax is unshifted when it is removed.[75] Combining this effect with the effects of imposing the VAT with its border tax adjustments, discussed above, results in a fall in the price of domestically produced goods relative to both imports in U.S. markets and foreign-produced goods in other countries. Thus imports should fall and exports should increase as a result of the tax substitution, provided the relevant elasticities of demand are large enough.[76] Of course, if the newly imposed VAT were not fully reflected in higher product prices, a trade improvement would result even under traditional assumptions of incidence of the corporation income tax, and if both exceptions to the traditional assumptions occurred, the favorable impact would be even greater. But given the downward inflexibility of wages, it seems unlikely that VAT would not raise prices. Thus it is unlikely that the tax substitution would improve the trade balance unless the corporation income tax is shifted (and would be unshifted when removed). Whether the corporation income tax is in fact shifted remains, as noted above, one of the unsolved riddles of economic analysis.

On balance, it is unlikely that the tax substitution would improve the balance of trade significantly. This is true if traditional incidence theory accurately describes the events that would follow the substitution. And even if the corporation income tax has been shifted,

---

[75] As noted above, the evidence from Krzyzaniak and Musgrave that the corporation tax is shifted does not also support unshifting.

[76] One estimate of the effect of such a substitution, assuming a given set of demand elasticities (imports: 1.0; exports: 2.0) is that a 5.65 percent VAT substituted for the corporation income tax would result in a $5.19 billion improvement in the U.S. balance of trade; see Maurice D. Weinrobe, "Corporate Taxes and the United States Balance of Trade," *National Tax Journal*, March 1971, pp. 79-86. Weinrobe also provides formulas for the calculation under alternative elasticity assumptions. The present author has also made estimates of balance-of-payments effects of substituting VAT for CIT in "The Economic Effects of Taxing Value Added."

as well it could have been, it probably would not quickly be unshifted. Unshifting might occur only as some prices rose less rapidly in the future than might have otherwise been the case. Thus on either account a substantial improvement in the trade balance seems unlikely.

An additional balance-of-payments effect of uncertain magnitude would result if reduction of the corporation income tax made the U.S. more attractive to investors. In such a case improvement on the capital account would occur. The uncertainty here derives from the complex effects of tax treatment of foreign investment income in various countries. Moreover, in large part the flows involved would represent an adjustment of stocks, and would be difficult to predict, as to both magnitude and duration, especially as they might be swamped by capital flows resulting from the recent devaluation of the dollar. On balance, some net inflow of capital would almost certainly result, but its size would be difficult to estimate.

F. Summary. The results of this section can be summarized briefly. Perhaps the first thing to notice is the unfortunate fact that nearly all conclusions about the economic effects of substituting the VAT for part of the corporation income tax depend upon the incidence of the latter tax, one of the great enigmas of economic analysis. The VAT is a neutral tax, if it is not riddled with exemptions, say to reduce its regressivity. On the other hand, the corporation income tax is distinctly nonneutral, especially if it is not shifted. It distorts choices of means of financing, factor proportions, form of business organization, industry mix, et cetera, besides resulting in double taxation of dividends (if not shifted). Yet if the corporation tax is not shifted, simple replacement of part of it with the VAT would not produce neutrality since the double taxation of dividends would be replaced by the nontaxation of retained earnings. Only integration of the two income taxes or increased taxation of capital gains would prevent introducing this distortion. But if the corporation tax is shifted, simply replacing part of it with a VAT would represent a distinct gain in economic efficiency. It will be seen in the next section that these questions of neutrality and distortion also play a role in the assessment of the distributional implications of the proposed tax substitution.

There can be little doubt that the tax substitution would increase the rate of private saving and investment in the economy, if the corporation tax is not shifted. If the tax is shifted, the tax replacement would not make much difference. Moreover, the VAT might be a better tool of discretionary fiscal policy than the corporation income tax, though it might not be as effective as an automatic stabilizer, again under the assumption that the latter tax is not shifted. If the corporation tax is shifted, it would be the better automatic stabilizer, but for discretionary use the taxes would be comparable. Finally, the tax substitution would probably raise prices initially by about the amount of the tax, the exact result again depending upon the incidence of the corporation tax. If so, not much improvement could be expected in the balance of payments. The possibility that adoption of the VAT would improve the balance of payments has, of course, been one of the chief advantages claimed for the tax.

5. Distributional Equity

Thus far we have considered the administrative advantages and dis-advantages of the value added tax and the likely economic effects of substituting the VAT for the corporation income tax. Now we turn to what many observers—particularly critics of the VAT—consider to be the crucial issue in the debate, the distributional implications of the VAT-corporate tax substitution. These, of course, revolve about the incidence of the two taxes, that is, who is burdened by them.

We noted above that a consumption type VAT would almost certainly be borne by individuals in proportion to consumption expenditures, but that the incidence of the corporation income tax is much less clear. Thus the best we can do is to consider the distributional implications of the tax substitution under two alternative assumptions about the incidence of the corporation income tax. As before, we assume alternatively that the tax is borne by shareholders and that it is shifted to consumers.[77]

If the corporation income tax is shifted to consumers, there is little reason on equity grounds not to substitute the VAT for it. In such a case the corporation tax is borne more or less in proportion to consumption in the aggregate, as the VAT would be if enacted. Yet it would be capricious in its incidence, given its nonneutral impact on various industries, (see section 4A above), and it might affect family budgets quite differently, depending upon consumption patterns. In short, if the corporation income tax is merely a tax on consumption, it is an extremely complex and nonneutral one that

[77] Backward shifting to labor, besides having little support from professional economists, would not result in a greatly different pattern of incidence than if forward shifting occurs, at least in the aggregate. Both patterns would differ little from the incidence of the VAT. Alternatively, the corporation tax would have about the same incidence as that of the payroll taxes, which are discussed in the next section.

could best be replaced by a relatively simple and neutral tax on value added (or a retail sales tax).

If the corporation income tax is not shifted to consumers, but is borne by shareholders, as traditional theory suggests, the question of replacing it in part with a VAT is more controversial. In this case we would be replacing a tax that contributes significantly to the overall progressivity of the American tax system with a regressive tax on consumption. Moreover, we would, as noted above, be creating a tax shelter in retained earnings. Whether such a step would be desirable depends in part upon society's views of equity in taxation and how the present tax system accords with them. Or, even if such a shift were thought by itself to be undesirable on equity grounds, it might be supportable if it would accomplish other economic objectives. In such a case we would be faced with a question of trade-offs between equity and the achievement of those other objectives.[78]

Some critics of both the nonneutrality of the present corporation income tax and the regressivity of the value added tax have offered an ambitious solution that would incorporate the best of both taxes. This solution would be to integrate the personal and corporation income taxes and make up the revenue lost in integration through a tax on value added.[79] The distortions inherent in the separate taxation of corporation income would be largely eliminated without creating a tax haven in retained earnings. The result would be a nearly neutral combination of (a) an individual income tax that included retained earnings and avoided double taxation of dividends and (b) a general tax on consumption. Such a policy could involve a rate structure that would leave more or less unchanged the overall progressivity of the tax system, or the rate structure could be adjusted to make the tax system more or less progressive, as desired.

A less extreme approach to avoiding creation of a tax shelter in retained earnings and its regressive incidence would be to combine replacement of the corporation tax by the VAT with a substantial tightening of capital gains taxation. In addition, it would be possible to mitigate the regressivity of the VAT at the lower end of the income scale by exempting purchases of basic necessities or providing refundable income tax credits to each family for the VAT on a given volume of purchases of basic consumer goods. Either approach would

---

[78] Krzyzaniak has argued persuasively, "Differential Incidence," that there may even be important conflicts between long- and short-run distributional objectives, in that egalitarian short-run policies may worsen the long-run position of low-income groups by reducing investment and the future capital stock.

[79] For a brief description of integration and references, see section 4B above.

reduce the VAT's regressivity, but from an economic viewpoint the refundable credit would be preferable to the exemption approach. The refundable credit would not distort choices between various items of consumption, whereas exemptions would discriminate in favor of the exempted items. Many critics of the simple replacement of the corporation tax with a VAT consider this dual approach of subjecting capital gains to more nearly full taxation and reducing the VAT burden on low-income consumers the least that should be done to lessen the regressivity of the tax change and make the substitution acceptable.

A more far-reaching approach would go beyond mere integration of the two income taxes. Integration would be supplemented by elimination of tax preferences under the income tax and initiation of low-income relief through something like a negative income tax.[80] Since the loophole closing would affect mainly upper income groups and the negative income tax would raise the disposable incomes of low-income households, the combination would greatly outweigh the regressivity of the VAT. Critics of this plan would object to the elimination of tax preferences or the payment of negative income taxes, or both. As always, equity is a matter of viewpoint and not of economic science.[81]

6. Comparison of VAT with Personal Income and Payroll Taxes

Up to now the economic and distributional effects of the VAT have been compared only with those of a corporation income tax. In this section we quickly make the same comparisons with the two federal

---

[80] The author has advocated this approach in his testimony before the Joint Economic Committee on March 21, 1972. For a further elaboration, see section 9 of this essay.

[81] It is of interest in this context to quote one observer's interpretation of policies accompanying Danish adoption of the VAT: "A modern variant [of the principle of tax neutrality] might be that a taxation reform would have to take into account, i.e., be neutral, as regards the existing 'social balance'. Such a relative neutrality of distribution has been maintained in connection with the introduction of the Danish value-added tax, steps having been taken to counteract its regressive effect by adjusting income tax rates; by introducing personal grants, which are inversely progressive in relation to income; by increasing the existing child grants; and by introducing subsidies granted to reduce the prices of certain dairy products. In this way we have obtained a system of direct and indirect negative taxes the avowed political objective of which is relative neutrality of distribution." From Mogens Eggert Möller, "On the Value-Added Tax in Denmark and the European Economic Community and the Renaissance of Tax Neutrality," *Bulletin for International Fiscal Documentation*, October 1967, p. 433, quoted in Shoup, "Experience with the Value-Added Tax in Denmark," pp. 240-41.

taxes that are more important sources of federal revenue than the corporation income tax, the personal income tax and the social security payroll tax. These comparisons deserve to be made since there is no a priori reason that only substitution for the corporation income tax should be considered. Certainly many opponents of the VAT would feel that if a VAT is inevitable it would be more palatable as a substitute for part of (an increase in) the payroll tax than for part of (an increase in) the corporation tax.[82]

Fortunately, the comparisons can be made quickly since in most cases the substitution would make relatively little difference, and the differences that would result are straightforward. This facility results from the fact that the incidence of these two taxes is itself fairly straightforward and more-or-less accepted, unlike the case with the corporation income tax. Economic theory suggests strongly that both the personal income tax and the payroll tax are borne by the income recipient involved, and there is as yet little empirical evidence to the contrary.[83] Thus in what follows it is assumed that both these taxes are borne by recipients of the taxed personal income or payrolls.[84]

A. Neutrality. Except to the extent that tax preferences in the individual income tax distort economic decisions and income taxation discriminates against saving, replacing part of that tax with a VAT

---

[82] On the other hand, many persons would argue against replacing the payroll tax financing of social security with any other tax, including a value added tax, because of the assumed similarity of social security to private insurance. For a thorough appraisal of the "insurance myth" and the economic effects of the social security taxes, see Joseph A. Pechman, Henry J. Aaron, and Michael K. Taussig, *Social Security: Perspectives for Reform* (Washington, D. C.: Brookings Institution, 1968) and the forthcoming volume by John A. Brittain, *Payroll Taxes for Social Security*, Brookings Institution.

[83] For a theoretical analysis of the situation in the short run, see the present author's "The Theory of Tax Incidence with Imperfect Factor Mobility." For a longer term view, see Krzyzaniak, "Differential Incidence," which also contains references to Krzyzaniak's various other writings on the subject. One empirical analysis of the incidence of payroll taxes, which supports the present author's theoretical presumption of incidence on workers, is John A. Brittain, "The Incidence of Social Security Payroll Taxes," *American Economic Review*, March 1971, pp. 110-25.

[84] It may be necessary to note explicity that both the employee's and employer's shares of payroll taxes are attributed to employees, as theory indicates they should be. To the extent that some or all of either share is passed on to consumers, replacing the payroll tax with a VAT would have no effect, and need not be considered explicitly. Thus the reader can interpret the analysis of the text as being applicable to whatever portion of the tax he believes is borne by labor, instead of by consumers.

would have little effect upon economic neutrality, so long as the latter is not riddled with exemptions; one neutral tax would be replaced with another. Of course, reduction of the existing personal income tax would mean that presently preferentially treated activities would be less favored than now by the tax law. Similarly, imposition of a VAT would favor any industries exempted from it. In this regard, it is worth noting that some important activities that are presently favored would probably continue to be favored, though perhaps not to the same extent. Housing is the most prominent example. Substituting VAT for part of the payroll tax would be neutral, except as exemptions in the former distort choices, since coverage of the latter is now nearing universality.

B. Growth. A tax on value added of the consumption type should be slightly more favorable to saving than the existing income tax for two reasons. First, being a regressive levy (see section 6E below), it takes income away from those most likely to spend it (and not save it), as compared to the income tax. Stated differently, the average of the marginal propensities to consume of those who would bear the burden of the VAT is greater than the average for the income tax. Second, because the VAT exempts saving and the income tax does not, substituting the former for part of the latter would lessen the disincentive against saving. How important these effects are is difficult to assess with any precision, but it seems that the differential impact of the two taxes on saving would be minor. Certainly, it should not be difficult to achieve the same increase in saving through less extreme means.

Similar conclusions hold for the substitution of the VAT for part of the existing payroll taxes, but the differential effects would be even smaller. Capital and labor would be treated equivalently under the VAT, whereas the payroll tax applies only to labor. Thus saving would become less attractive. But the impact flowing from the redistribution of tax burdens and differences in marginal propensities to consume would be quite insignificant. Thus, in total, it seems unlikely that much added saving could be expected from either of the tax substitutions considered in this section.

Similarly, there seems to be little reason to expect any dramatic shifts in risk-taking, innovation, and investment because of these tax substitutions. As with the corporation income tax, the personal income tax results in governmental sharing of both risks and returns, and may either stimulate or retard investment from a given flow of saving. In either case the expected results are not great, and for the payroll tax they are even less. In total, then, it does not seem likely that either potential tax substitution would appreciably affect the rate of economic growth in the United States.

C. **Stability.** As in the discussion of section 4D, the effects the postulated tax substitutions would have on the achievement of full employment and price stability can be considered in three stages: the initial and direct effects of the substitution upon the level of prices, the relative effectiveness of the tax alternatives as built-in stabilizers, and the usefulness of the taxes as instruments of discretionary countercyclical policy.

First, it seems likely that removal of either the personal income tax or the payroll tax would have little effect upon prices. On the other hand, the newly imposed VAT would probably be reflected in higher prices. Thus the initial effect of the substitution would probably be an increase in the price level about equal to the rate of the VAT.

The effectiveness of the various taxes as built-in stabilizers depends upon the response of receipts to cyclical deviations from the target path of GNP and the impact these changes in receipts would have upon private spending. VAT receipts would respond less than receipts from the payroll tax and much less than those from the personal income tax. But by the very same token that VAT receipts, being based on consumption, may be relatively insensitive to fluctuations in income, fluctuations in income and payroll tax receipts may induce little change in private spending. In either case, consumption behavior based on permanent income, rather than upon contemporaneous income flows, is the culprit. Private spending may be sufficiently insensitive to near-term alterations in income that none of the three taxes would be a strong built-in stabilizer. Thus there seems to be little reason to prefer one of the taxes over the other on the grounds of contribution to automatic stability.

As a tool of discretionary fiscal policy, the VAT seems to have a slight edge over its two direct tax alternatives. From an administrative standpoint all three could be altered with comparable ease.[85] But the effect of the temporary change in the VAT would probably be considerably stronger, especially if the tax measures were known

---

[85] It would be necessary to allow the President to alter VAT rates within preset limits for countercyclical purposes, as noted in section 4D. Otherwise, anticipatory buying and postponement of buying of consumer durables would create perverse effects while the measure was being debated, since tax rate changes might be fairly large.

to be temporary. Experience with the 1968 income tax surcharge suggests that temporary income tax changes are reflected in altered consumption only gradually and with a considerable lag, on the average. Therefore they must be planned well in advance and tailored closely to stabilization needs.[86] There is no reason to believe that consumption would respond very differently in the short run to a temporary change in the payroll tax.

On the other hand, a temporary change in a tax on consumption, precisely because it is temporary and is geared to consumption, rather than to income, can be a quite effective tool of discretionary fiscal policy. Besides simply reducing private purchasing power, as do changes in the income and payroll taxes, the change in the VAT would create a strong incentive to postpone or speed up purchases in order to make them under the lowest possible tax rate. This intertemporal substitution effect is, of course, missing under the income and payroll taxes, since these taxes apply to the earning of income rather than the spending of it.[87] Thus, the VAT would probably be a better instrument of discretionary stabilization policy than either the income tax or the payroll tax.

In summary, the initial replacement of part of either the personal income tax or the payroll tax with the VAT would almost certainly lead to prices rising by the amount of the tax on value added. The VAT would probably be a more powerful tool of discretionary stabilization policy than either of the direct taxes, but as automatic stabilizers the three taxes would probably not differ much in effectiveness.

D. Balance of Payments. Imposition of a VAT in place of part of the personal income tax or payroll tax would not be likely to affect the balance of payments significantly. Reduction of either direct tax would not affect domestic prices, but imposition of the VAT would

---

[86] One appraisal of the 1968 surcharge is presented in Arthur M. Okun, "The Personal Tax Surcharge and Consumer Demand, 1968-70," *Brookings Papers on Economic Activity*, 1971(1), pp. 167-204. A more pessimistic view is taken in Robert Eisner, "Fiscal and Monetary Policy Reconsidered" and "What Went Wrong." The present author has reviewed fiscal policy during the 1960s in *Fiscal Failure: The Lessons of the Sixties* (Washington, D. C.: American Enterprise Institute, 1972).

[87] This intertemporal substitution effect is discussed in William H. Branson, "The Use of Variable Tax Rates for Stabilization Purposes," mimeographed, 1971. It is proposed there and in McLure, *Fiscal Failure*, pp. 67-71, that attention be given to a variable tax-subsidy arrangement related only to consumer durables (and investment), rather than to all consumption spending, since it is for these large durable items of expenditure that we would expect the intertemporal substitution to be the greatest.

raise them by the amount of the tax. However, the VAT would be rebated on exports and applied to imports, so that exports would occur free of the tax and imports would compete on an equal footing with domestic products (so far as the U.S. VAT goes). Thus little or no improvement would be expected to occur in the trade account because of the tax substitution. There might be some inflow of capital in response to lower personal income tax rates, but it would probably be an insignificant amount. Of course, lower payroll taxes would have virtually no effect on the capital account.

E. Distributional Effects. The most dramatic effects of substitution of a VAT for the personal income tax would be the shift toward regressivity that would occur in the incidence of the U.S. tax system. Though it is riddled with loopholes, the personal income tax is a markedly progressive element of the U.S. tax system, especially over some income ranges. The VAT, on the other hand, being a general tax on consumption, would be a regressive levy. Even if exemptions were allowed for housing, medical expenses, household utilities, and food, as they well might be (see section 3 above), the incidence of the VAT would probably fall short of proportionality. Thus substituting a value added tax for part of the personal income tax would be to substitute a regressive tax for a progressive tax, a result surely unacceptable in many quarters. Just how great the shift toward regressivity would be would depend upon the exemptions in the VAT and the form of the personal income tax reduction. A fully general VAT would be more regressive than one with liberal exemptions for basic necessities, as noted above. Of course, a refundable credit for a fixed amount of VAT paid on basic necessities would be a preferable means of reducing the regressivity of the tax, as noted in section 4B. A uniform percentage reduction of personal income tax liabilities would lessen progressivity more than an equal reduction in all tax rates or a further increase in personal exemptions, et cetera.[88]

The distributional implications of substituting a VAT for part of the payroll tax would not be great, in the aggregate. The VAT

---

[88] It should be noted that none of these methods of reducing the personal income tax would benefit those families presently exempt from the tax. To extend to them, the "tax reduction" would have to take the form of initiation of (or an increase in payments under) a negative income tax. These families would, of course, pay part of the VAT, unless the refundable credit were granted. The distributional implications of raising additional revenue through a VAT and various other taxes is examined in Charles L. Schultze, Edward R. Fried, Alice M. Rivlin, and Nancy H. Teeters, *Setting National Priorities: The 1973 Budget* (Washington, D. C.: The Brookings Institution, 1972), pp. 440-48.

would probably bear slightly more heavily on the lowest income groups than the payroll tax, due primarily to its inclusion of the consumption of low-income persons not taxed heavily by the payroll tax. The most important group in this category is the aged. Thus in one sense the tax substitution, while distributionally roughly neutral in the aggregate, would result in an income transfer from nonworkers to workers, in particular from the aged to the young and middle-aged members of the labor force. In the last respect it would offset in part the transfer from the young to the aged resulting from the social security system.[89]

F. Summary. The rates of saving, investment and economic growth, the neutrality of the tax system, the automatic stability of the economy, and the balance of payments probably would not be affected much by substituting a tax on value added for part of either the personal income tax or the payroll tax. The VAT should be a somewhat stronger tool of discretionary fiscal policy than either of the others, but its initial substitution for them would raise prices. Replacement of part of the payroll tax with a VAT would not affect the distribution of real income much in the aggregate, but it would result in a transfer from consumers as a group to workers as a group. The most important social aspect of this transfer would be the added burden on the aged living on pensions and social security. If the substitution were for part of the personal income tax, the overall incidence of the federal tax system would move toward regressivity.[90] The extent of the shift would depend upon the exact form of the income tax reduction (equal percentage reduction in liabilities, equal percentage point reductions in rates, increase in exemptions, initiation of a negative income tax, et cetera) and whether steps were taken to reduce the regressivity of the VAT (via exemptions or refundable credits for the VAT that hits basic necessities). If a general VAT were matched with an equal percentage reduction in all personal income tax liabilities, the shift to regressivity would be substantial indeed, and probably the most important effect of the tax substitution.

7. VAT and the Property Tax

President Nixon has suggested that the United States should consider initiating a federal tax on value added, the revenues from which would

---

[89] See Brittain, *Payroll Taxes for Social Security.*

[90] It should be mentioned that an offset would occur due to the deductibility of state and local taxes in calculating liabilities under the federal income tax. Reduction of rates would reduce the value of these deductions in terms of tax saving.

be used to relieve the burden of the local property tax, presently the primary local source of financing for education. The details of any such proposal are not at all clear at this time. But given the successful attack on property tax financing of education in recent court cases, it seems essential that our study should at least consider in broad outline the effects of substituting revenues from a federal tax on value added for those currently being raised by the local property tax. This section briefly examines these effects, the analysis following the same approach as above. No effort is made to investigate in depth all the many ramifications that adoption of such a proposal would have for the financing of federalism.

A. Neutrality. Like the federal corporation income tax, the portion of the property tax levied on improvements is distinctly nonneutral.[91] It does not necessarily discriminate between industries, as the corporation tax does, but it discriminates between geographic areas.[92] Because of the political fragmentation of the nation at the local level there are literally thousands of taxing jurisdictions, each with its own property tax base and rate. Far from having uniform rates, many of these jurisdictions have been created, and are perpetuated, precisely to provide preferentially low tax treatment of property within their boundaries. And even when differences in taxation have not been the conscious goal of public policy, different property tax bases and revenue requirements and faulty local assessment practices have resulted in uneven taxation. Thus we can expect substantial distortion in the geographic location of economic activity to result from the lack of uniformity of the property tax. This distortion is likely to be greatest within a given metropolitan area since locational choices as between cities are likely to be made on nonfiscal grounds.[93]

One of the most adverse effects of the property tax is the disincentive it imposes upon private efforts to rebuild the decaying central cities of the nation. The result is the hastening of flight to the suburbs and the worsening of urban blight, which in turn renders more difficult the financing of urban public services via the property tax in the central cities.[94]

Finally, and this can be considered under the heading of both income distribution and resource allocation, reliance upon the property

---

[91] The portion levied on land is, of course, neutral since it affects no economic decisions at the margin.

[92] Interindustry distortions may occur, however, depending upon the law and assessment practices in various states.

[93] See Netzer, *Economics of the Property Tax*, especially chapter 5.

[94] Ibid., pp. 83-85.

tax for the financing of education results in vastly differing resources being devoted to a child's education, depending upon where he lives. If there are benefits to society from the education of its children and future citizens, as is usually assumed and as is implicit in public support of education, it seems to make little sense from the viewpoint of resource allocation to provide such divergent levels of education for these children. Moreover, the court cases mentioned earlier have ruled that such divergent levels of support for education within a state are unconstitutional.

Replacement of the portion of the local property tax that is imposed upon improvements with revenues from a tax on value added would eliminate most of these distortions of resource allocation.[95] The VAT would apply at uniform rates across the nation and therefore would not distort locational decisions. Similarly, it would be neutral with regard to decisions of central city renewal. Finally, if revenues from the VAT provided a uniform minimum grant per student, educational differentials would probably be reduced. Even if they were not, students in areas with inadequate property tax bases could be provided education of a satisfactory quality to meet social demands. Thus it seems likely that the proposal would improve resource allocation.[96]

B. Growth, Stability and Balance of Payments. Presumably the replacement of part of the property tax, a tax on capital, with a tax on consumption would raise the rate of growth somewhat, though this consideration should probably not be important in the decision to make the change. Similar comments apply to the built-in stability of tax revenues and the balance of payments. Revenues from a VAT would be somewhat more variable over the cycle than those from a property tax.[97] It seems unlikely that the VAT rate would be varied over the cycle if receipts from it are tied closely to the financing of education. Finally, part of the property tax on improvements may be

---

[95] Because the portion of the property tax levied on land does not cause distortions, as noted above, there is no need (on efficiency grounds) to replace it. Equity considerations are taken up in section C below.

[96] It might be noted that elimination of the property tax on housing and exemption of housing under the VAT would accentuate the existing preferential treatment of owner-occupied housing under the income tax. On the other hand, income tax deduction for property taxes on homes would no longer be so bothersome.

[97] It probably would not be desirable to allow the variation in revenues to be reflected in variations in the amount of funds available for support of education. Stable revenue flows could be achieved in several ways, and need not be discussed here.

shifted to consumers, in which case the proposed tax substitution would result in both a rise in the price level of less than the amount of the VAT and a slight improvement in the balance of payments. None of these effects seems to be very important, however, especially when compared with the implications for neutrality and income distribution.

C. **Distribution.** It has been estimated that the property tax is markedly regressive over the lowest income brackets, and regressive even at high-income levels if the offset against the federal income tax is taken into account.[98] This regressivity results from the large portion of the tax falling on housing and the portion shifted to consumers.[99] Since the part of the tax levied on land is almost certainly more progressive than that on improvements, there is little doubt that the portion on improvements is itself regressive, and distinctly so at the lowest income levels. Whether the VAT or the property tax (on improvements) is more regressive is not clear, but there is one big difference in the two taxes. The property tax bears especially heavily upon housing, while the VAT would probably exempt it. This consideration is especially important for the aged, who in many states pay large property taxes on their homes but would pay relatively small amounts of VAT.[100]

Finally, we must turn briefly to an issue that until now we have been able to avoid—the distribution of the benefits of public expenditures, in particular those of education. It is possible, if not certain, that education would be financed more generously under a VAT than under continued major reliance upon the property tax. If so, it is worth noting that the regressivity of the VAT would probably be more than offset by the pro-poor distribution of benefits from education. On the other hand, it can be argued that financing the same pro-poor benefits through increased federal income taxation, rather than through a federal sales tax, would be even more advantageous to the poor. Whether the level of financing would be equally high under the VAT and the income tax is an open question.

---

[98] Netzer, *Economics of the Property Tax*, chapter 3.

[99] Of course, if the tax on improvements is borne by capital, rather than by consumers, the result is quite different. For a discussion of this difficult theoretical problem, see Peter M. Mieszkowski, "The Property Tax: An Excise Tax or a Profits Tax?" *Journal of Public Economics*, March 1972, pp. 73-96.

[100] It should be noted that the property tax causes distortions primarily as it affects new construction. Similarly, removing the tax on existing real property would create windfall gains to present owners. It may be preferable to phase out the property tax by not applying it to newly made improvements rather than simply removing it.

D. Summary. It seems that a VAT would be far less distorting than the property tax, and that its incidence by income brackets would not differ too much from that of the property tax. The incidence of both taxes would, however, depend crucially upon the family's market basket, in particular upon its consumption of housing, since the property tax hits housing especially hard and the VAT would probably exempt it. This distinction is particularly important for the aged. Considerations of growth, economic stability, and the balance of payments should probably play a distinctly minor role in the discussion.

Finally, it should be questioned whether a VAT is the proper tax to substitute for property tax financing of education, if a substitution is to be made. There seems to be little reason to prefer the VAT to a retail sales tax. Moreover, some critics of the VAT would support transfer of educational financing to the federal income taxes rather than to either type of general sales tax.

8. The VAT in Europe [101]

Among the questions that naturally arise when one is considering the adoption of a federal tax on value added in the United States are "how is it done in Europe?" and "what have been VAT's effects in Europe?" This section provides a brief and necessarily incomplete answer to these questions.

The first VAT in Europe was adopted by France in 1954. But this tax extended only through the wholesale level, and the French extended the tax to the retail level and to services only on January 1, 1968, the date Germany substituted a value added tax for its notoriously defective cascade type turnover tax. Thus the Danish VAT, adopted as a replacement for a tax levied at wholesale in July 1967, was the first truly general VAT in Europe. Other European nations utilizing this tax are the Netherlands and Sweden (1969), Norway and Luxembourg (1970), and Belgium (1971). Italy, after numerous delays, was scheduled to implement a VAT in mid-1972, the year of Ireland's proposed initial use of the tax, but has been given a further extension until January 1, 1973. Finally, Britain and Austria have also announced proposals to adopt a VAT in 1973.

Only Denmark and Norway have adopted single-rate taxes on value added, though the disadvantages of multiple-rate systems are well known. (Sweden nominally has one rate, but it applies the tax

---

[101] This discussion is taken largely from National Economic Development Office, *Value Added Tax*, pp. 31-50, and "VAT in Europe," pp. 64-65.

to a reduced tax base.) Germany, the Netherlands, and Luxembourg have two rates and both France and Belgium have four rates. (See Table 6 for a compilation of existing and proposed rates. (The proliferation of rates is apparently attributable to union resistance to higher rates on essential goods and services than existed under previous tax systems. Not surprisingly, the reduced rates (and exemptions) apply primarily to items that might reasonably be considered necessities: food, housing, transportation, electric utilities and telecommunications, newspapers, and social and medical services. Conversely, differentially high rates apply primarily to luxury items —which in effect means automobiles. In this regard it has been noted that "Possibly by coincidence, the single-rate countries are also those with the most developed social welfare systems, and the most progressive direct tax scales; as a result they least need to attempt income redistribution via high VAT rates on luxuries and low ones on necessities."[102] Finally, the financial sector is usually exempt on the services it provides, though not on its purchases. In a similar vein, those in certain activities can choose whether or not to be in the VAT system, and thus able to take credit for taxes paid on purchases.

It is difficult to generalize about the economic effects of the adoption of the tax on value added in Europe. Effects on the efficiency of resource allocation are not directly observable, and can only be surmised from theoretical arguments and the nature of the pre-existing tax systems. Where the VAT replaced a cascade type turnover tax, as in Germany, Luxembourg, and the Netherlands, the gains in economic efficiency are almost certain to be great. On the other hand, where it replaced a retail sales tax, as in Norway and Sweden, or even a wholesale tax, as in Denmark, the gains are not likely to be so important. Where it replaced a variety of indirect taxes, as in Belgium and France, an intermediate result is likely. Since in no case has the VAT replaced an important direct tax (except in France, where the social security payroll tax was eliminated), the European evidence on this score would be of little relevance to the U.S.

Similar statements can be made about the effect of adoption of a VAT on the rates of saving and investment. First, the effects probably would not be large since the VAT replaced primarily other indirect taxes. Second, the effects would be difficult to isolate, even using sophisticated econometric techniques, since the initiation of the VAT occurred in the context of economic growth. Finally, the rele-

---

[102] "VAT in Europe," p. 64. The passage quoted in footnote 81 of section 5 about the maintenance of relative neutrality of distribution when the VAT was introduced in Denmark supports this view.

Table 6
RATES OF VALUE ADDED TAXES IN EUROPE

	Date of Introduction	Taxes Replaced	Rates (percent)			
			Standard	Lower	Intermediate	Upper
France	1968	Various indirect	23	7.5	17.6	33⅓
Germany	1968	Cascade	11	5.5	—	—
Italy*	1973	Various indirect	?	?	?	?
Belgium	1971	Various indirect	18	6	14	25
Netherlands	1969	Cascade	14	4	—	32
Luxembourg	1970	Cascade	8	4	—	—
Denmark	1967	Purchase tax	12.5	—	—	—
Norway	1970	Retail sales tax	20	—	—	—
Sweden	1969	Retail sales tax	17.65	3.53	10.59	—
Austria*	1973	Cascade	16	8	—	—
Ireland*	1972	Purchase tax + retail sales tax	16.37	5.26	9.82	30.26
Britain*	1973	Purchase tax	10	0	—	—

* proposed

Source: "VAT in Europe," *The Economist*, March 25, 1972, p. 65—with the exception of the dates for Italian and Dutch adoption of VAT. Italy has been granted an extension until January 1, 1973 and the Netherlands adopted VAT in 1969, not 1968, as *The Economist* reports.

vance to the U.S. consideration of a federal VAT is limited, in any event, as noted above.

Probably the single question asked most often about the European taxes on value added is how they affected prices when they were introduced. The answer to this question is crucial for the likely effects on the balance of payments, as well as in its own right. Here the evidence is mixed. Germany was perhaps the most successful in its efforts to prevent a large increase in the price level from accompanying its introduction of the VAT. It is generally agreed that the substitution of the VAT for the German cascade tax had little effect on the price level. France was only slightly less successful in that less than 1.15 percent inflation has been attributed to the VAT. In Luxembourg and the Netherlands the price increases associated with the introduction of the VAT have been estimated at 2.0 percent and 1.5 percent, respectively. These increases occurred in spite of a freeze on prices, as did the 5.8 percent price increase that has been attributed to the Norwegian tax on value added. The worst price increase was that in Denmark—7.9 percent, but this increase was mitigated by a general increase in wages and special relief for low-income persons.[103]

Again, most of this European experience is not directly relevant to an appraisal of the likely effects of the introduction of a federal tax on value added in the United States, since in most cases the VAT replaced indirect, rather than direct, taxes. (The most analogous case is that of Norway, in which a switch from direct to indirect taxation occurred simultaneously with introduction of VAT. In that instance a price increase of almost 6 percent—as compared to a VAT rate of 20 percent—occurred.) Because European experience is not directly relevant to the U.S., it is necessary to rely on theoretical analysis. As was indicated earlier, it is probably safe to say that the impact of the introduction of the VAT itself would be to raise prices by about the percentage amount of the tax. Only if the corporation income tax (or another direct tax) had been shifted forward in the form of higher prices and would be unshifted when reduced, as seems to have been roughly the case for the indirect taxes replaced by the VAT in all the European countries except in Norway and Denmark, could we expect prices not to rise markedly with introduction of a VAT. If the corporation tax is not shifted, or if it would not be unshifted when reduced, prices would probably rise by about the amount of the tax. Similarly, the balance of payments probably would not improve if the corporation tax is not shifted or if it is shifted

---

[103] National Economic Development Office, *Value Added Tax*, pp. 43-45.

but would not be unshifted. Only if the corporation tax operates exactly like an indirect tax could we expect much improvement in the balance of trade from the tax substitution.

9. Concluding Remarks

Most of the discussion to this point has been relatively free of normative judgments, as indeed it should be, in order that the author's views on equity, neutrality, et cetera, and the trade-offs between them would not intrude. An attempt has been made simply to establish the likely economic and distributional implications of various possible tax substitutions, and the areas of substantial uncertainty, without expressing any preferences on how the various implications should be valued. In this final section, a normative framework for weighing the implications of substituting VAT for other taxes and the author's personal views on the policy alternatives outlined in this essay are described.

A. A Normative Framework. Which aspects of the substitution of VAT for various other taxes should count most in determining whether the United States should adopt a tax on value added? To answer this question, it is necessary to analyze what can be done only (or most directly) by tax policy and what can be done in other ways, the idea being that judgments of the desirability of an American VAT should be framed primarily in terms of the former. The discussion of the desirability of a VAT should center on the issues of neutrality and equity. Distortions introduced by a tax such as the existing corporation income tax can hardly be undone, except by replacing the tax with a truly general tax and taxing retained earnings, and to try to offset these distortions in any other way would greatly complicate our economic system. Similarly it would be extremely difficult to offset existing inequities in the distribution of income except via taxes and transfers related to income, and newly imposed taxes working in the opposite direction would only worsen the problem.

On the other hand, one can think of many measures to increase the rate of economic growth, stabilize the economy, and improve the U.S. balance of payments. For example, one can increase the rate of saving in the economy, if that is a factor, by increasing the government surplus (assuming that full employment can be maintained). If lagging innovation and investment pose a problem, they can be subsidized directly. Though it is more difficult to stabilize the economy than to talk about doing it, the basic structure of the tax system should not be dictated by the needs of stability, without regard for the efficiency of resource allocation or the distribution of income. A similar argument applies to improving the balance of payments, as recent events have shown. Something as important as the basic nature of domestic tax policy should not be made to hinge upon the need to protect the international strength of the dollar.

Thus we come to the basic question of whether the gain in neutrality that would result from substituting a VAT for part of the corporate income tax is worth the reduction in progressivity that would result. No answer can be given to this question at a technical level, but several things should be kept in mind in making the choice. First, if the corporation tax is now shifted, there seems to be only one answer: the more neutral VAT should be adopted in place of the equally regressive corporation income tax. Second, the substitution would not result in true neutrality unless taxation of retained earnings were part of the substitution. But (assuming no shifting of the corporation tax) that would also mean that the regressivity of the tax change would not be as great as if a simple substitution were contemplated. Thus the conflict between neutrality and progessivity is not as great as appears at first glance. Third, regressivity at the lower end could be reduced by allowing exemptions for basic consumer goods. But since these exemptions would distort consumption choices a preferable means of reducing regressivity would be to allow a refundable credit for a fixed amount of value added tax payments or to initiate low-income relief directly, say through a negative income tax. Finally, the regressivity of the VAT could be more than overcome while eliminating further distortions by combining with it the integration of the corporate income tax, income tax reform, and low-income relief.

With regard to the choice between the VAT and the personal income tax, the choice itself is a matter of value judgment, but the basis for the choice seems fairly clear. The taxes are probably about equally neutral, so the decision can be made on the basis of equity. There is perhaps even less to choose between the payroll and value added tax. Both are more or less neutral, and their incidence by income brackets may not differ too much. But the payroll tax favors recipients of capital income and retirement income relative to consumers and recipients of labor income.

As regards the proposal of a federal VAT to replace the local property tax as a source of financing education, the issues again are clear. The property tax is distinctly nonneutral, whereas the VAT is, at least in principle, a neutral tax. The primary question on the equity side involves the differentially heavy taxation of housing under the property tax and the likely exemption of housing under the VAT. Moreover, some critics of the VAT would argue that the property tax burden should be relieved by sharing revenues from an increase in the federal income tax, instead of those from a newly imposed federal sales tax.

Finally, it should be noted again that virtually any effect of a tax on value added can be achieved by imposing a tax on retail sales rather than the VAT. In fact, many of the questions of economic effects examined in this essay can more easily be answered in the context of the familiar retail sales tax than in the context of the relatively unfamiliar VAT. That the U.S. should impose a VAT, and not a federal retail sales tax, if it should decide to impose either, should be decided on administrative grounds rather than being taken for granted.

B. Author's Personal View. I have tried to be objective in presenting the pros and cons of the various tax substitutions discussed in the main body of this study, though I have almost certainly fallen somewhat short of complete success. It is, after all, difficult enough to tolerate opinions we cannot share; to play them back accurately and without prejudice is even more demanding.

In this short section I wish to state my own views on the questions discussed in the study, if only because I am often asked what they are. The reader may find this statement of opinion useful, so that he can better detect how my views have infiltrated the allegedly objective presentation of pros and cons. In any case, in this statement I need no longer feel encumbered by the mantle of objectivity.

First, it should be obvious that no simple answer can be given to the question of whether the U.S. should adopt a VAT. As is so often the case in the field of tax policy, the answer depends upon what tax the VAT would replace and the context in which the replacement would occur.

The combination I would prefer would involve integration of the personal and corporate income taxes, closing of loopholes in the newly integrated income tax, and initiation of low-income relief. Such a package would eliminate the distortions created by the existence of a separate corporation income tax, but without removing retained earnings from the tax base. Moreover, it would provide relief at the bottom of the income scale, without introducing exemptions and the distortions they entail. Finally, the added progressivity resulting from income tax reform and low-income relief would make the regressivity of the VAT bearable, especially since the rate structure could be adjusted in the interest of equity.

In the context of a thorough overhaul of the tax system, such as the one described above, the reduction of the property tax on improvements would be attractive. The property tax is a particularly unsatisfactory tax, whose demise would not be widely mourned. I have argued elsewhere that if federal financing were rationalized as suggested above, the property tax could be replaced by general local taxes on sales or income or by shared revenues from a federal VAT, a federal retail sales tax, or the federal income tax.[104]

If one were to stop short of this rather radical tax reform, a VAT might still be acceptable if accompanied by the proper measures. Substitution of the VAT for the corporation tax would probably be acceptable *if* the taxation of capital gains were tightened and relief were provided to low-income families through a refundable credit against their income tax liabilities. Simple substitution without these additional measures would, however, not be acceptable. The tax shelter in retained earnings would be unacceptable on both equity and efficiency grounds. Similarly, imposition of a VAT in place of part of the corporation income tax without low-income relief would be unacceptable on equity grounds, and relief through exemptions, while barely acceptable on equity grounds, would distort choices too much to be acceptable on neutrality grounds.

Substitution of the VAT for the personal income tax or payroll taxes would represent no great gain in neutrality, but by the same token it would be acceptable on efficiency grounds. On the other hand, the equity implications of replacing part of the progressive personal income tax with a regressive VAT are unacceptable. Replacing the payroll taxes with a VAT would be acceptable, though it would not represent a great leap forward in equity.

Next, I would not find the proposal the President has outlined particularly objectionable. Elimination of the property tax on improvements would, I think, be a step forward, and perhaps even a large one. On the other hand, the equity implications do not seem to be too bad since the property tax is itself probably a regressive levy.[105] Moreover, the net effect of substituting the VAT for property tax financing of education might be to equalize the sum of net real income

---

[104] Charles E. McLure, Jr., "Revenue Sharing: Alternative to Rational Fiscal Federalism," *Public Policy*, Summer 1971, pp. 457-78.

[105] But some reduction of the preferential income tax treatment of owner-occupied housing would seem to be in order in this case.

and the value of education (though not as much as if the income tax, rather than the VAT, were substituted), since the proposal should improve education most where it is now the worst. That result, of course, depends crucially upon the formula chosen for sharing the revenue from the VAT. (A flat per student allocation seems to be the most sensible.)

It will have been noted that in this statement no mention has been made of the effects of a VAT on the rate of growth, the stability of the economy, or the balance of payments. This silence reflects the viewpoint, expressed in section 9A, that equity and neutrality should be the key considerations in judging basic changes in the tax structure of a country, with other considerations assuming only minor roles. These other factors are important, and all the implications of adopting a VAT would need to be watched so that policy adjustments could be made for them, but they should not control the decision.

Finally, although the discussion thus far in this statement of personal views has been in terms of a VAT, I personally would prefer (though not strongly) that the federal government adopt a retail sales tax, if it is to adopt either form of general sales tax. The two taxes should be economically equivalent, so that the decision can be made on administrative grounds. I believe that these support a preference for the retail tax, though there is room for considerable disagreement on that score. One thing is clear about the choice, however: it should be based on a far more careful assessment of the two alternatives than has surfaced to date.[106] The choice should not go by default to the VAT because no one bothered to ask the question.

---

[106] Due, "The Case for Retail Sales Tax" and Shoup, "Value-Added Tax in Denmark" are, of course, excellent statements of the issues by experts. But few people indeed are familiar with the points discussed in them.

ECONOMICS OF THE VALUE ADDED TAX

Norman B. Ture

Introduction and Summary

The subject of the value added tax (VAT) has commanded increasing attention in the United States over the past several years, primarily in the academic and business communities. Much of the interest in the tax lies in the possibilities it might afford, by virtue of border tax adjustments, for improving the nation's international trade balance and in its superiority over the income tax as a means of taxing business. Moreover, the fact that the tax is the central revenue raising device in the fiscal harmonization of the European Economic Community and that several other countries in Europe and in Latin America have adopted the tax inevitably raises questions as to whether the United States would not do well to introduce a VAT into its revenue system.

More recently, consideration of the VAT has gained in urgency as a result of the substantial federal deficits in fiscal years 1971-73. The rapid rate of increase in federal spending, combined with forecasts which suggest that present taxes even at full employment will provide less revenues than projected outlays, has impelled a search for new revenue. And in the past year an additional source of urgency is the developing crisis in financing public education that results from recent court decisions challenging the constitutionality of the local property tax funding of public schools. If federal financial aid is to be provided localities to replace property taxes, substantial federal revenue increases in all likelihood will be required. Reducing property taxes, widely characterized as regressive, and bolstering local governments' financial resources for education might well be regarded as appropriate occasions to add a VAT in order to augment the federal inventory of taxes. This possibility, hinted at by the President in his January 1972 State of the Union message and publicly discussed by various administration officials, brought the VAT to the front pages of the nation's newspapers.

To date, unfortunately, most of the discussion in the press and in popular forums has had the tone of an adversary proceeding, convicting the VAT of fiscal crimes before affording it a fair trial. The VAT is generally labeled a national retail sales tax. Bearing the label of a sales tax, it is then characterized as regressive on the assumption that all sales taxes bear more heavily on the poor than on the affluent. Moreover, it is asserted that imposition of the VAT would be inflationary, raising the prices of consumption goods and services across the board. These are, of course, important issues, but they deserve more objective treatment than the *ad hominem* assertions which are so frequently made. A fair appraisal of the tax by the general public is made even more difficult by discussing it as an alternative to local property taxes, thereby confusing the issues pertinent to the VAT with other issues such as the extent to which the federal government should assume responsibility for public school financing and difficult questions as to the incidence of property taxes.

The relevant issues raised by the proposal for a federal VAT concern the correct characterization of the tax, its impact, shifting and incidence, its distribution by income level, and its likely economic effects. These issues should be examined separately from the question of what public expenditures the VAT might finance. In a nutshell, the relevant question is whether a VAT would be a better tax for the federal government to impose than those it now relies upon. Or if federal revenues must be increased, would it be better to raise additional funds by imposing a VAT rather than by increasing the rates or broadening the base of one or more existing taxes?

It is argued in the discussion which follows that the VAT, properly structured, is not a "consumption" tax but a proportional tax on payments for the service of factors of production. The VAT would not raise the general level of prices. Compared with existing federal taxes, it is far more nearly neutral in its effects on consumption and saving and on the mix of labor and capital services used in production. Compared with the income tax, it would lead to a larger stock of capital used with labor in production and would thereby enhance labor's productivity and real earnings. As a corollary, the

U.S. balance of trade would in time show a larger surplus (or smaller deficit) if a VAT rather than income taxes were relied upon to raise any given amount of revenues. The VAT would not be regressive; the distribution of VAT liability by income level would be substantially the same as the distribution of labor and capital income.

On these grounds, this discussion concludes that substituting the VAT for the present income taxation of business would be a major step toward constructive tax reform. Moreover, the substitution should be undertaken irrespective of whether federal fiscal requirements exceed the revenues to be expected from existing taxes. In this event, business income taxes should nevertheless be reduced with the VAT supplying both the revenue foregone plus such additional revenues as may be desired.

1. What Is a Value Added Tax?

To begin with, we should be sure of what the VAT is—that is, what is the base of the tax?

As the name suggests, a VAT is a tax on the value added during the course of a business's operations to the goods or services it sells. In the simplest terms, the amount of value so added is measured by the difference between the dollar amount of the firm's sales and its purchases from other firms. Simple arithmetic shows that this difference is precisely equal to the payments the business makes for the labor and capital services it uses in its operations, i.e., to the sum of its payroll and "profits."

There are varying versions of a VAT, but the one which has engaged our attention and is most widely used elsewhere is the so-called "consumption" version.[1] In this version, a business in calculating its VAT base deducts from its net sales all of its purchases from other businesses—raw materials, semi-finished goods, finished goods for resale, fuel, power, light, office supplies, and the amount of its purchases of capital facilities, e.g., plant, machinery, equipment, store and office furniture and machines, etc. Because it deducts the cost of production facilities in the year in which they are acquired, the business claims no other deduction for depreciation, depletion, or other form of capital consumption allowance. Its tax base, to repeat, is equal to its net sales less all of its purchases from other firms. Simple arithmetic shows that this base is equal to the amount it pays for the labor it hires and its profits, where profits are adjusted

---

[1] I use the term "consumption" merely to conform to popular usage. As I shall show later, the tax is not on consumption.

by adding back any capital consumption allowances and by subtracting any change in inventory and outlays for production facilities.[2]

The national income variant of the tax differs in one major respect. Instead of subtracting the full amount of capital outlays from the base in the year in which these outlays are made, a capital consumption allowance (depreciation and/or depletion) is permitted. In this version the "profit" component of the tax base is very much the same as under the present corporation income tax.

The third principal version of the tax is the so-called gross national product variant, under which no deduction whatever is allowed for capital outlays, either in the year in which these outlays are made or over a period of years in the form of a depreciation or depletion allowance.

Of these three variants of the VAT, only the first, the so-called "consumption" type, should, in my judgment, be given serious consideration. This type of VAT most closely conforms to the criterion of neutrality as between consumption and saving and as between the use of labor and capital services in production.[3] The "national income" version retains the bias of the present income tax against saving and capital, and the "gross national product" version increases that bias manyfold.

In the remainder of this discussion, all references are to the so-called consumption version of the VAT.

2. Exemptions

One of the advantages claimed for the VAT by some of its proponents is that, at least in theory, the tax should apply unexceptionally to all economic entities, in the business sector, the household sector, and in the public sector as well. The theory behind this view is simplicity itself. The base of the tax is the sum of the payments made by an economic entity for the factors of production it uses. In an efficiently operating economy these payments are at least roughly equal to the value of the products those factors of production would supply in their best alternative uses. These payments are therefore a pretty fair measure of the opportunity cost to the economy as a whole of the economic entity's particular use of the factors of production it

---

[2] A number of other adjustments to the income tax measure of profits are also required. Principal among these is to add gross proceeds from the sale of any and all assets and to ignore entirely any gain or loss on the sale of capital assets. In addition, dividends received are not included in the VAT base.

[3] That is to say, imposition of the VAT does not change the relative cost to any individual of consumption and saving nor the relative cost to any producer of using labor or capital production inputs.

employs. And every economic entity using factors of production, and thereby depriving the rest of the economy of their use, imposes that same sort of cost, no matter what its production consists of. Accordingly, there is no basis for exempting any economic unit from the tax.

Moreover, applied without exception, the tax minimizes distortions in the allocation of resources. Since the base of the tax is value added in production, equal to the cost of the productive services used therein, its universal application would not differentially affect production costs among companies, industries, or lines of activity. Hence, the levy would not induce taxpayers to alter proportionately the use of their resources, the exercise of their claims for consumption or saving, or the composition of their market baskets or investment portfolios. Any exemption erodes this neutrality and should, on these grounds, be resisted.

Opponents of the VAT counter by asserting that, as a practical matter, exemptions would be provided and that, as a consequence, the tax would become an administrative nightmare and in the process lose much of its claim to superiority on neutrality grounds. This possibility, of course, should not be ignored. On the other hand, exemptions are not an intrinsic or necessary feature of the tax, and surely the administration and Congress are not required to emasculate a VAT by riddling it with exemptions.

If a VAT is to be adopted with exemptions, these should be severely restricted. Households might be exempt on the ground that total value added in the household sector, hence the VAT liabilities thereupon, is so small as to fall short of the administration and enforcement costs attributable to this sector. It is unlikely that the federal government would impose a VAT on itself, and almost equally unlikely that the tax would be imposed on states and localities.

No other exemptions than these would be warranted. It is often urged that certain categories of production, such as food, clothing, housing, and medicine, should be exempt to overcome the allegedly regressive impact of a VAT. The argument is based on the assumption that the VAT is a sales tax, its burden resting on consumers. But the VAT is, in fact, a tax on payments for factors of production, not a tax on the consumption of commodities and services. As such, there is no more reason to exempt from the VAT the value added in the production of food, say, than there is for exempting from the present payroll taxes the wages paid to labor in the food growing, processing, and distributing industries, or to exempt from income tax the profits of companies engaged in these activities.

With exemptions limited to value added in the government, household, and institutional sectors of the economy, the VAT base in the U.S. in 1971 would have been about $756 billion.[4] The exemption of value added in the production, processing, and distribution of food would have reduced the tax base by about $50 billion; exempting rent on low- and middle-income housing would have eliminated another $30+ billion from the base; and the exemption of medical and other health services and of educational services would have brought the VAT base down by another $39 billion. In other words, the exemptions of these economic activities would have cut the VAT base by roughly $120 billion, a little less than one-sixth, to about $636 billion.

Of course, additional exemptions, however unwarranted on analytical grounds, might be afforded, or as sometimes proposed, the alleged regressiveness of the VAT might be ameliorated by an income tax credit for low-income taxpayers. The VAT's annual revenues, thus, might range from a high of $7.6 billion per percentage point of tax to a low of, say, $6.0 billion. To put these revenue yields in perspective, a 5 to 6 percent VAT would have generated the same revenues as the federal corporation income tax (measured in the national income accounts) in calendar year 1971.

3.   Methods of Computing and Collecting

The mechanics of computing and collecting the VAT has commanded much attention in popular discussions of the tax. Indeed, the method used in most countries—the credit or invoice method—seems to be largely responsible for its widespread characterization as a sales tax.

In fact, there are three basic, alternative methods for computing the tax: the addition method, the subtraction method, and the invoice or voucher method. The addition method calls for adding up all the payments made by the business for the production services it uses— its payroll and profits—and subtracting from that amount (1) the change in inventories and (2) capital outlays.[5]

---

[4] This estimate assumes that roughly half of the value added in residential construction that year would have been embodied in rental property. Calculations of the VAT base for 1971 are shown in the technical note. Data are from U.S. Department of Commerce, Bureau of Economic Analysis, *Survey of Current Business*, April 1972.

[5] For this purpose, profit is adjusted by adding back any capital recovery allowances and other special deductions allowed for income tax purposes, and by subtracting certain other receipts included for income tax purposes, e.g., dividends and net gains or losses.

The subtraction method requires the taxpayer to calculate his total net sales and receipts (excluding dividends and gains or losses but including gross proceeds from the sale of capital assets) and to subtract from this total all of his purchases from other businesses, including his capital outlays.

For either the addition or the subtraction method, virtually all of the information required to compute the tax is included on the present income tax forms and supporting records. No new information is called for; no record-keeping other than that now required for ordinary business financial statements is needed. Either quarterly returns (as in the present payment system) or a single, annual return, with supporting records, would provide all the necessary documentation, and the return itself could be completed on a very short form. Complying with any tax is burdensome, but these two methods of computing the VAT involve far less of a chore for the taxpayer and the tax administrator than does the present income tax.

The third method—the invoice method—is the one used in virtually all of the countries having a VAT. Under this method the taxpayer applies the VAT rate to the amount of his sales and shows this amount of tax as a separate item on his sales invoice. Every business making purchases from other businesses, therefore, finds the amount of the tax on each such purchase separately stated on the invoice he receives. To compute the amount of tax he pays the government, he adds up all the VAT he has "charged" his customers, subtracts all the VAT his suppliers have "charged" him, and the remainder is his VAT liability.

It is frequently assumed that the invoice method will be proposed for use in the United States. The principal advantage claimed for this method is that it is self-enforcing: to establish the correctness of his own VAT liability each taxpayer would have to show the amount of tax he "paid" in his purchases from other businesses, and he would want to be sure that he "passed on" to his customers the amount of tax owing on his sales, which his customers presumably would insist on seeing separately on their purchase invoices for the same reason. However valid this method may be for other countries, its use is not obligatory in the United States. U.S. taxation is based on significant differences in tradition, custom, history, compliance, and enforcement machinery. The compliance record of U.S. taxpayers is excellent, and there is no reason to believe that it would not continue to be so with respect to the VAT.

If exemptions and/or differential rates were to be provided, compliance would be less burdensome under the invoice than under the subtraction method. Under the invoice method, it is clear, each taxpayer would need only his purchase and sales invoices to determine the amount of tax to remit to the Treasury. Under the subtraction method, however, the taxpayer would have to segregate his purchases by VAT rate in order to determine how much of these purchases were deductible. For example, suppose wheat growers were not required to remit VAT, but the value of the wheat was nevertheless to be included in the VAT base at the next production stage, say the miller. Under the invoice method, the miller would have no VAT on his purchase invoice to deduct from the VAT on his sales invoices; the latter would automatically include the VAT payable on both the wheat growing and milling value added. Under the subtraction method, on the other hand, the miller would have to know that wheat purchases were not deductible. If numerous exemptions or rate differentials were provided, therefore, compliance would be more cumbersome under the subtraction method than under the invoice method. Of course, this argument is as valid in reinforcing the case against exemptions and differential rates as in supporting the invoice rather than the subtraction method.

The invoice method, by requiring a separate notation on each invoice of the amount of VAT ostensibly generated by each sale, conveys and reinforces the incorrect notion that the tax is passed forward in full from one production stage to the next. As we shall see later, what is meant by "passing the tax forward" is by no means clear. Suffice it is say at this point that the VAT required to be shown on any given invoice is not the seller's VAT liability with respect to that sale; as we have seen, his liability is the amount he shows on his invoice *minus* the VAT amount he has "paid" to his suppliers on his purchases. In fact, his VAT liability can be determined only at the end of the taxable period when he takes into account all of his purchases, including capital goods, from other businesses. The invoice method, thus, misrepresents the amount of tax due on the value added by each seller.[6]

If for no reason other than to avoid the impression that the VAT is automatically shifted forward to the final consumer, the invoice

---

[6] One counter argument addressed to this point is that the VAT is not intended to be a tax on the company, measured by the value added in its business, but a tax on the value of the final product, i.e., a retail sales tax collected at each production stage up to and through the final sale. Thus, it is maintained, every business is supposed to "pass the tax forward," acting only as a collection agency. Indeed, it is contended, in this view of the tax the company's profit and loss statement should be completely unaffected by the VAT. In the subsequent discussion we show that irrespective of the accounting procedures prescribed for the VAT, it must in fact affect the real cash flow of virtually every business.

method should not be used for a VAT adopted in the U.S. The subtraction method is just as easy to comply with; indeed, in many cases, it might well be easier, and it much more readily identifies for the taxpayer the elements in his business operations which affect his VAT liability.

A. Border Tax Adjustments. Earlier, it was noted that the VAT is imposed on imports and rebated on exports. Assuming that any VAT adopted by the U.S. would include these border tax adjustments, the mechanics would be relatively simple.

In the case of imports, the VAT would be applied, at the same rate applicable to value added in domestic production, to the full value of the imports as reported to the Customs Bureau as the imports entered customs. In the case of exports, the U.S. exporter would deduct the invoice value of export sales from his total net sales and receipts before deducting his purchases from other businesses in arriving at his taxable value added, assuming the subtraction method is used for computing the tax. Under the invoice method the taxpayer has no VAT liability on his export sales and claims a credit for all of the VAT shown on his purchase invoices.

4. Burden

When we talk about the burden of a tax, we ask who is "worse off" because the tax is imposed. So far as the VAT is concerned, there is a broad consensus that its burden rests on consumers. Presumably, the tax is "passed forward" by the producers and sellers at each production stage until the full amount of the accumulated tax is included in the price of consumer products and services in their final sale. Consumers bear the burden of the tax, so the argument goes, because the prices of the consumption goods and services they buy are higher by virtue of the VAT.

The discussion that follows attempts to demonstrate that this assignment of burden is incorrect. The burden of the VAT is not on the act of consumption, hence not on consumers. Rather, the tax rests, as suggested above, on the costs incurred in production, hence on the incomes gained by the factors of production.

A.   Why Call VAT a Consumption Tax? To begin with, let us critically examine the contention that the burden of the VAT rests on consumers, i.e., that the VAT is a consumption tax.

It is far from clear what is intended by characterizing the VAT as a consumption tax. In nontechnical discussions, the "consumption tax" or "retail sales tax" characterization of the VAT appears to derive in large part from the method of assessing the tax used in European countries. Under the so-called invoice or credit method, as described above, each business "charges" its customers a VAT equal to the tax rate times the value of the sale. To determine the amount of VAT it is to remit to the government, each business subtracts the amount of VAT it has been "charged" by its suppliers from the amount of VAT it has "charged" its customers. Superficially, the VAT collected in this way appears to be a sales tax with an offsetting credit for the tax paid on the business's purchases.

This method of computing and collecting the tax, of course, tells us nothing about its burden. As suggested above, the invoice method conveys the impression that every producer-seller passes the tax forward. Suppose this were true. Would it mean that the VAT burdened only consumers and that producers were unaffected by the tax?

It is clear, of course, that the imposition of the VAT does not increase either consumers' or producers' income or wealth; no one has more money because the tax is levied. If every producer-seller were to pass the tax forward, what would consumers, with no more income or wealth than before, do when they observed that the prices of every consumer good and service had been increased by the accumulated amount of VAT? Presumably, they would reduce the physical volume of their purchases of such goods and services. But if they were to do so, then the tax has resulted in a reduction in the physical volume of sales and, unless producers are willing to build inventories endlessly without prospect of increasing sales, in the physical volume of production as well. But if the amount of goods and services produced decreases, so too must employment of the factors of production, unless businesses are willing endlessly to pay for labor and capital services they are not using. And if employment of these production inputs is reduced, so too must be the incomes of those who provide the labor and capital services. But then the burden of the tax is not uniquely on people as consumers; it is borne also by those who contribute to production in the form of a reduction in incomes received for supplying production inputs.

But suppose it is argued that consumers will not reduce the physical amount of their purchases in response to the increase in prices resulting from the imposition of the VAT. With no increase in income or wealth, if people were to buy the same physical quantity of consumer goods and services and pay more for them, then clearly they would have to reduce their saving, and by an amount equal to the VAT "passed forward." This argument, thus, leads to the startling conclusion that this alleged consumption tax actually is a tax solely on saving.

In technical discussions, the consumption tax characterization of the VAT seems to rest on the argument that since purchases of capital goods are deductible from the tax base, the tax bears only on the value added in the production of consumer goods. In the aggregate, the base of the tax—ignoring any exemptions—is asserted to be equal to the value of final sales of consumer goods and services.[7] Hence, it is argued that VAT is merely a cumbersome way of collecting a tax on the retail sales of consumer goods and services.

Assuming that some useful purpose is served by applying distinctive names to various taxes, the label "sales tax" or "consumption tax" is not appropriate for the VAT. On semantic grounds, the base of a sales or excise tax is the value of the sales (or the number of units sold). The base of the VAT, as we have seen, is the difference between the value of sales and the value of purchases from other businesses, which for any taxpayer is equal to the amount of his payments for the labor and capital services he employs.

It might be argued that the VAT is an excise on the firm's production costs. There is merit in this characterization just as there is in labeling virtually any tax an excise on the taxed subject or thing. A payroll tax is an excise on one component of production—the cost of labor services—just as a profits tax is an excise on another component —the cost of capital services. An income tax is an excise on using one's resources to generate income measured in the market, and an estate or gift tax is an excise on certain property transfers. For many analytical purposes, treating every tax as an excise is highly useful, but for purposes of quickly identifying familiar things we find it more useful to apply different names to the various taxes. If for no other reason, naming the VAT a sales or consumption tax is misleading and interferes with an objective and constructive evaluation of the tax.

On analytical grounds, the characterization of the VAT as a consumption tax is simply wrong—not merely a matter of semantic confusion. The VAT does not single out consumption as the object to be taxed. The VAT does not differentially burden consumption

---

[7] The assertion is wrong unless specific exemptions are provided not only for value added originating in the government sector but also for the value added generated in the production of goods in the private sector for sale to governments. See the calculations of the VAT base in the technical note.

compared with saving. The VAT does not tax people in their role as consumers and exempt them as savers-investors. The VAT does not differentially affect the prices of consumption goods and services as compared to production goods and services.

As repeatedly suggested earlier, it is more accurate to characterize the VAT as a tax on the opportunity costs imposed by the taxpayer in his employment of production services. The immediate impact of the VAT is on the business's payroll and "profits"; it is, in short, a combination of a payroll and a profits tax. If some label other than VAT is necessary or desirable, perhaps "consolidated business tax" would be most appropriate.[8]

B. How to Characterize a Tax. It is clear, of course, that every tax reduces the private sector's claims over production resources and their outputs. Every tax, thus, is intended to reduce the taxpayer's spending on something, either his purchases of goods and services for consumption, his purchases of claims to future income, his purchases of real assets which will generate income for him over an extended period, or all of these purchases in some degree or other. The fact that any particular tax results in less spending for consumption than would occur in the absence of the tax does not justify labeling the tax a consumption tax, unless it can be shown that the tax disproportionately reduces consumption outlays relative to other uses of income. In evaluating the consumption tax characterization of the VAT, therefore, the critical question is whether the tax reduces consumption outlays in greater proportion than it reduces savings or capital outlays.

The ultimate effects of any tax depend on its initial impact in changing relative prices and on how people respond to these changes. Since every tax changes the price of something(s) relative to the price of other things, the nature of the adjustments in the economy to the imposition of the tax depends on the character and the extent of the response to this relative price change, i.e., on the price elasticity of the "thing" on which the tax initially impacts. When the shifting process, i.e., the adjustment to the imposition of the tax, has been completed (or substantially so), one may compare the new state of affairs with that which existed before the imposition of the tax and characterize the incidence of the tax in terms of the differences between the two. Thus, if in a post-tax equilibrium, a smaller proportion of private sector claims is used for consumption than in the pre-tax

---

[8] Mr. John Englested, chairman of the board of the O. S. Walker Co., suggested this as a better, more descriptive name for the tax. Only its acronym suffers in comparison with "value added tax."

economy, one could describe the tax as a "consumption" tax. Or, if after the responses to the imposition of the tax were substantially completed, one found that the real income of the "poor" had been reduced in greater proportion than that of the "rich," one might characterize the tax as regressive. Or if one found, in comparing the pre-tax and post-tax equilibrium situations, that there were less capital services in use relative to labor services in production generally, one could characterize the tax as burdening capital.

In truth, it is difficult to make these comparisons in a dynamic economy in which many things are continuously changing and in which the data required to isolate the effect of a tax are most elusive. While it is a relatively simple matter to identify the nature of the change in relative prices associated with the imposition of the tax, to delineate the kinds of adjustments which will occur because of this change in relative prices, and to define the conditions under which no further changes in economic activity will occur, it is extraordinarily difficult to measure these changes. As a practical matter, therefore, most discussions of the shifting and incidence of taxes depend on heuristic analysis. The quality of such analysis depends critically on how accurately the initial price impact of the tax is identified.

With this preface concerning analytical methodology, let us return to the question of the impact and incidence of a VAT. In the following discussion it is shown, first, that the VAT is not a consumption tax but falls in equal proportion on consumption and saving. Secondly, it is demonstrated that the VAT does not differentially affect the prices of consumption goods and services and of capital goods and services.

C. **Effects on Consumption and Saving.** To begin with, let us imagine an economy without taxes and with efficiently operating markets. Every decision-making individual in the economy allocates his income between current consumption and saving on the basis of his preferences between present consumption and future income. The more of today's income he saves, the larger will be his income tomorrow. The amount of the increase in his future income depends on the "interest" he receives on his saving (the amount of "interest" he receives is determined by his and everyone else's preferences as between present consumption and future income, i.e., the supply of saving, and the productivity of the capital in which savings may be embodied). Given the rate of interest he finds in the market, each individual determines how much of his current income to consume and how much to reserve for increasing future income.

Clearly his (and everyone's) consumption-saving choice is influenced by a host of factors. But given all these influences, the amount he consumes and saves depends on the relative cost of consumption and saving. The cost of consumption, of course, is the amount of future income foregone; similarly, the cost of saving is the amount of consumption and the satisfaction therefrom which the saver must forego. When the individual has allocated his income between consumption and saving optimally, given his preferences, that relative cost is equal to the interest rate he finds in the market.

If the relative cost of savings and consumption is changed, the individual is likely to change the proportion of his income which he saves. Thus, if a tax is to fall neutrally, i.e., with equal proportional impact on consumption and saving, it must not alter their relative cost. A tax which raises the relative cost of saving, then, may be characterized as a tax on saving. Similarly, a tax which raises the relative cost of consumption, hence reduces consumption by a larger proportion than it reduces saving, may be fairly characterized as a consumption tax.

Coming back to our taxless economy, let us assume that it is decided to impose a flat-rate tax on everyone's income, where income for tax purposes is measured as including current saving. Suppose the tax rate is, say, 50 percent. Before the tax was imposed, a person needed $1 of current income either for $1 of current consumption or for an income of $.10 per year in perpetuity (assuming the "interest" rate is 10 percent).[9] With a 50 percent income tax, he needs $2 of current pre-tax income to finance $1 of current consumption, but he needs $4 of pre-tax income for a perpetuity of $.10 after-tax income.[10] Thus, while the income tax at 50 percent has doubled the cost of current consumption, it has quadrupled the cost of saving, i.e., of buying the same amount of future income in this form. Clearly, the tax has reduced the relative cost of consumption or, equivalently, raised the relative cost of saving. Following the suggestion above, the tax should be characterized as a tax on saving (although, to be sure, both consumption and saving will be reduced), since it has increased the cost of saving relative to consumption.

---

[9] The amount he would have to pay for this $.10 per year income is given by the expression for the present value of a perpetuity $A\infty = \dfrac{Y}{r}$, where Y = the annual income and r = the interest rate.

[10] Since the "interest" earned on his saving is also taxable at the 50 percent rate, he needs to save $2, on which his after-tax "interest" will be $.10. To save $2, he needs a pre-tax income of $4.

It is often argued that private saving is insensitive to changes in the rate of interest and that, accordingly, it is little if at all affected by tax provisions which increase its cost relative to the cost of consumption. If this were the case, it would mean that consumption would decline in greater proportion than saving in response to the imposition of an income tax of the sort described above. But surely this is a highly unlikely proposition, for it asserts that when the cost of consumption is *reduced* relative to the cost of saving, *less* rather than more consumption—as a proportion of income—results. (By the same token, if the relative cost of consumption were increased, consumption presumably would increase rather than decline, according to this proposition.)

Now suppose that the tax which is to be imposed on the initially taxless economy allows a deduction for current saving, taxing the "interest" on that saving as it is earned. If the taxpayer spends $1 for current consumption, he needs $2 of current, pre-tax income. But if he wished to forego that $1 of current consumption in order to have a perpetuity of $.10 per year, he needs only $2 in pre-tax current income, not the $4 required in the case of the income tax.[11] In this case the 50 percent tax has increased the cost of current consumption by 100 percent, and it has increased the cost of saving, i.e., of future income, by the same percentage. In other words, the relative cost of saving and of consumption has not been affected by the tax. The tax which allows a deduction for saving from current income, therefore, is neutral as between consumption and saving.

To be sure, both consumption and saving are likely to be reduced by the tax. But if we assume that the taxpayer had optimally allocated his income between consumption and saving, he will not presumably alter that allocation after the tax (which allows the deduction of savings) is imposed, since, as shown, that tax does not alter the relative costs.

A VAT of the so-called (and misnamed) "consumption" variety falls between the two taxes sketched above. As described, the VAT would indeed allow deductions for saving to the extent that saving was embodied in businesses' purchases of production facilities, increases in inventory or other real assets, i.e., elements included in the national income accounts measure of "gross private domestic investment." But other private saving, particularly that embodied in human capital which is erroneously treated as consumption spending, might

---

[11] To have an income of $.10 per year, after tax, he needs $.20 per year pre-tax. Since, by hypothesis, his saving would be deductible for purposes of *this* tax, he needs only $2 of pre-tax current income to pay for the perpetuity.

well remain subject to tax unless specific provision were made for the deduction of such saving. To the extent that the VAT were to apply to factor incomes where these incomes included returns to human capital, for which no deduction had been allowed at the time the saving therein embodied was made, the VAT would not be perfectly neutral as between consumption and saving but would retain some bias against saving. Compared with the present income tax, however, the VAT would represent a major step toward neutrality with respect to consumption-saving choices, and away from the tax bias against saving and capital formation.

D. Impact on the Cost of Consumption and Capital Goods. One of the popular (and mistaken) allegations about the VAT is that since the taxpayer deducts his purchases of production facilities in arriving at the base of his VAT, the cost of capital services is exempt from the tax. Hence, it is maintained, the VAT rests only on consumption goods, i.e., increases the cost of consumption goods and services but not the cost of capital services.

As I have attempted to show, the VAT is not properly character-ized as a consumption tax; it does not increase the cost of consump-tion relative to saving. Then what, indeed, is the burden of the VAT?

As shown earlier, the direct impact of the VAT is to increase the cost to producers of using production inputs. For any company, the VAT base is equal to its sales less all of its purchases from outsiders, which is the same as the sum of its payroll plus its profits, less its change in inventories and net addition to its production facilities. Clearly, the initial impact of the tax is on the payments made for factors of production employed by the firm, i.e., the payments the firm makes for the services of the labor and capital it employs. Since these payments are also the incomes of those providing the labor and capital services, the VAT is properly viewed as a proportional tax on the income of the factors of production employed by the taxpayer.

The deduction for purchases of the facilities which provide capital services does not remove the cost of these services from the VAT base; rather, it places the taxation of the payments for these services on an equal footing with the taxation of the payments for other production services. On the other hand, failure to allow the deduction of capital outlays, as in the income tax, results in imposi-tion of the tax first on the capitalized value of all the services to be generated by the capital at the time the capital facilities are acquired and subsequently on the payments for these services as they are

84

provided over time. Nondeductibility of capital outlays, thus, results in a compounding of the tax on the payments for capital services and raises the cost of using these services relative to the cost of other production inputs. Permitting the deduction for capital outlays at the time they are made, by the same token, confines the application of the tax to the gross returns for the capital's services as these returns are generated over time. The VAT does not exempt capital from taxation but merely taxes payments for capital services at the same rate as payments for other factors of production. (It is, thus, neutral with respect to the tax burden it imposes on the use of all production inputs.)

To illustrate: in the absence of a tax, a firm wishes to purchase $X of production facilities. It needs to allocate thereto $X of its own income (or $X of outsiders' incomes if the outlay is to be externally financed). To warrant the outlay, the present value of the net returns allocable to the facilities must be at least equal to the price of the facilities, $X. Thus, in equilibrium in efficient markets,

$X = A_r^N Y$, where

$A_r^N =$ the expression of the present value of an annuity of $1 for N years, discounted at r percent; and

$Y =$ the annual income allocable to the facilities, i.e., the amount the facilities must earn if the owner(s) of the company is (are) to provide the $X of saving to the company for the purchase of the facilities. In other words, Y is the annual payment for, or cost of, the capital services provided by $X of capital facilities.

Now suppose a VAT were imposed, allowing a deduction for capital outlays but no depreciation deduction from the annual income attributable to the facilities purchased by these outlays. The gross earnings of the facilities now bear a tax each year $= tY$, and the annual after-tax earnings are $Y - tY = Y(1-t)$, the present value of which is $A_r^N Y(1-t)$. With no change in r, however, an annual income of $Y(1-t)$ will not warrant the outlay of $X for the facilities. The annual pre-tax income of the facilities will have to increase sufficiently so that after paying the tax, Y remains, i.e., $Y_1 = \dfrac{Y}{1-t}$, where Y_1 is the pre-tax amount which the facilities must earn if $X are to be provided for their purchase. For example, if X = $1,000, Y = $100, and t = 20 percent, Y_1 must equal $125.

The deductibility of capital outlays under the VAT, therefore, does not exempt capital goods from the tax. On the contrary, VAT increases the cost to the company of using capital services and in the same proportion as it increases the cost of using other production inputs. For example, if before the tax, L man-hours of labor service were employed at an hourly rate of w, these labor services would have to contribute $wL=W$ to the company's revenues. If the same amount of labor services are to be employed at the same hourly rate after the tax is imposed, their pre-tax contribution to revenues will have to increase sufficiently so that the after-tax amount, $W_1(1-t) = W$, where $W_1 =$ the required pre-tax contribution to revenues. In other words, W_1 must $= \dfrac{W}{1-t}$. Thus, the tax increases the cost of using labor services in the same proportion as it increases the cost of using capital services, i.e., by $\dfrac{1}{1-t}$.

E. Effects on the Price Level. One of the fiscal crimes of which the VAT is widely accused is that it raises the price level. Often this charge is based on casual observations rather than analysis. It is frequently contended, for example, that where the VAT was adopted in Europe, the price level promptly rose. An examination of the facts shows no consistent pattern of change in the price level in relation to the rates of the VAT. A closer relationship emerges between changes in the price level and in the stock of money. Looking at the following table, the general conclusion one should reach, it seems to me, is that increases in the money stock, not the introduction of the VAT, account for the increases in the price level.

It is possible that the use of the invoice method by most of the countries which have adopted the VAT contributed to a temporary surge in prices. Since this method instructs the taxpayer separately to show and to add the VAT to his sales invoices, it is plausible that business quite generally did so without adjusting the base sales price at first, until they had had the opportunity to see the effect of these increases on their sales. In time, however, prices must have adjusted so that they generally were about in line with the level which basic monetary, fiscal and market conditions dictated.

Apparently, the conviction that the VAT raises prices is of a piece with the view that it is a tax on consumption and/or a tax that is passed along from production stage to production stage until it comes to rest on the consumer. I have attempted to show earlier that the tax would be neutral with respect to the relative cost of consumption and saving and is not therefore properly characterized

Table 1
MONEY, CONSUMER PRICES, AND THE VAT IN EUROPE

Country	VAT Rate(s) at Date of Adoption	Percentage Change	
		From 4th qtr. preceding adoption of VAT to date of adoption	From date of adoption of VAT to 4th qtr. after adoption
Belgium	6%, 15%, 20%, 25% [a]		
Money		.07	n.a.
Consumer prices		.03	n.a.
Denmark	10%		
Money		.09 [b]	.17 [c]
Consumer prices		.08 [b]	n.a.
Netherlands	4%, 12% [d]		
Money		.10	.08
Consumer prices		.08	.03
Norway	20%		
Money		.05	.05
Consumer prices		.09	.07
Sweden	11.11%		
Money		−.08	.02
Consumer prices		.02	.06
West Germany	5%, 10% [e]		
Money		.02 [f]	.10
Consumer prices		.03 [f]	.02

[a] Each of the four VAT rates is levied on different, specified items. A basic rate of 18% is levied on items not specifically taxed at one of these rates.
[b] 4th quarter 1966 and 4th quarter 1967; VAT adopted 3rd quarter 1967.
[c] 4th quarter 1967 and 4th quarter 1968; VAT adopted 3rd quarter 1967.
[d] 12% on most items; 4% on food, etc.
[e] 10% on most items; 5% on food and agricultural products, etc.
[f] 4th quarter 1966 and 1st quarter 1968; VAT adopted 1st quarter 1968.
Source: International Monetary Fund, *International Financial Statistics*, vol. XXIV, no. 9, September 1971.

as a consumption tax. But let us consider from another point of view the contention that the tax is passed on and hence raises prices.

The argument that the VAT would raise prices appears to be that since every business, presumably, would pay the tax, each business would pass on the tax it pays to its customers. The raw material producer would pay its tax on the amount of its value added and presumably include that tax in the price it charges the, say, manufacturer which buys those raw materials. The manufacturer, in turn, would deduct from its net sales the full cost, including tax, of its purchases from the raw material producer, and pay the value added tax on the difference. It would, supposedly, add its value added tax to the price of its output when it sells that output to, say, a wholesaler. And so on down to the ultimate consumer.

But could every business pass along to its customers the full amount of its VAT liability? Could the prices of all products and services sold to consumers increase by the full amount of the tax?

All prices could be raised enough to pass the tax along fully only if there were a general inflation just because the VAT was imposed. And this could come about only if our monetary authorities were to increase the money supply sufficiently to allow all prices to rise. Hopefully, the Federal Reserve Board would not follow this course. If the Federal Reserve were to hold to a steady course of money expansion, prices generally could go up only if the amounts of goods and services offered for sale decreased. If the physical volume of sales goes down—or rises more slowly than otherwise—so does the physical volume of production and so does, therefore, the use of the factors of production, labor and capital. But if employment and the use of capital rise more slowly than otherwise, in time, wage rates and profits will rise more slowly than otherwise. And in time, for that very reason, prices generally will be lower than otherwise.

This analysis leaves us with this conclusion: if the money supply grows no faster than it would have in the absence of a VAT, the imposition of a VAT cannot generally and permanently raise prices.

This is not to say that no company or industry would be able to pass the VAT along to its customers in the form of higher prices. As we all know, some prices can be raised with little loss in sales, and these prices would be raised to pass along the VAT. But other prices would come down. The overall result, in time, must be the same price level which would prevail given basic monetary and market determinants.

F. The VAT as a Proportional Income Tax.

As we have seen, the deductibility of capital outlays does not exempt the payment for capital services from the VAT; rather, the tax applies at the same rate as on a company's payments for labor services. Thus, if a company were paying $W per unit of labor services (L) and $Y per unit of capital services (K), its VAT liability would be $t(\$WL + \$YK)$. With given market prices of labor and capital services, the VAT obviously increases their cost to the user.

If the company is to continue to use the same amount of these production services and to pay the same market price per unit, it is clear that its total revenues from the sale of the goods or services they produce must increase, i.e., the price of the output must rise. The amount of the required increase per dollar is $\dfrac{t}{1-t}$. Thus if $t = 20\%$, a product that formerly sold for \$1 must now sell for \$1.25.

The question whether the VAT could be fully and directly "passed forward" in higher prices was examined above and it was concluded that the VAT itself could not raise the general level of prices, that such inflation could occur only because of untoward monetary expansion, and that such monetary expansion was not an essential accompaniment of the adoption of a VAT. Let us suppose that the stock of money (or the change therein) is not affected by the introduction of the VAT. Under these circumstances, if the same amount of production services is to be employed, the market price per unit of these services, i.e., their incomes, clearly will have to fall (or at least rise less rapidly than otherwise). If the prices of these production services are sticky downwards, i.e., either do not fall or rise as rapidly as in the absence of the tax, fewer of these production services will be employed. As before, the aggregate income of the suppliers of these services will be reduced.

Next, assume that monetary expansion permits increases in product prices to "pass the tax forward," so that the same amount of production services will be employed at the same market prices as before the tax. Now the increase in the price level with the same market prices of production services means that the *real* incomes of those supplying these services must fall.

The conclusion that the tax must reduce real income, of course, is not unexpected. Every tax must have this effect. A tax which failed to do so simply would not be a tax at all, i.e., it would not affect the total volume of real claims available to the private sector and therefore would not transfer any real claims to the government. What distinguishes the VAT from other taxes, however, is that it falls in equal proportion on all incomes.

G. Is the VAT Regressive? The point has been made repeatedly in the preceding discussion that the VAT is a proportional tax on the incomes of factors of production. The popular view of the tax, on the other hand, is that it is regressive. This assertion apparently is based on the view that the VAT is a tax on consumption and that consumption represents a declining fraction of income as income increases. Hence, the lower the income, the greater the ratio of VAT paid to income. As shown earlier, VAT is not a consumption tax, either in the sense that it is passed on from producer to consumer or in the sense that it increases the cost of consumption relative to saving. In some more sophisticated discussions, the charge that VAT is regressive appears to rest on the assertion that capital is exempt from the tax and that the distribution of capital ownership is skewed toward the rich. However, as shown, capital is not exempt from the VAT, but is taxed on equal terms with other production inputs.

A third basis for the allegation that the VAT is regressive arises in connection with proposals to substitute the VAT for the income tax on corporations. In this case, it is sometimes explicitly conceded by the VAT critic that the VAT is in fact a proportional income tax, but it is maintained that the corporation income tax is progressive in the income-level distribution of its burden. Hence, it is argued, a substitution of the VAT for the corporation income tax represents a switch from a progressive tax to a proportional tax, i.e., a move toward regressivity. This contention clearly rests on the characterization of the corporation income tax as a progressive income tax, a matter which lies beyond the immediate purview of my discussion. Suffice it to say that there is hardly a consensus as to the ultimate incidence of the corporation income tax. Indeed, many VAT critics are persuaded that the corporation income tax is largely "passed forward" to consumers, a conviction which surely must undercut this basis for opposing a substitution of the VAT for the corporation income tax. Until there is a sturdier empirical demonstration than is now available of the impact and incidence of the corporation income tax, one cannot confidently compare this tax with the VAT from the point of view of regressivity.

5. Capital Formation and Productivity

Just as criticism of the VAT often exceeds the constraints of carefully reasoned analysis, advocacy of the tax is sometimes more enthusiastic than is warranted. This exaggeration is nowhere so clear as in the case of the claims made on behalf of the VAT with respect to private capital formation.

In most instances, the favorable impact of the VAT on investment is attributed to the alleged exemption of capital from the tax. But, as shown above, the VAT does not exempt capital but merely avoids the compounded taxation of capital imposed by an "income" tax.

If we go back to our example of the initially taxless economy, we find that the imposition of the VAT will increase, in equal proportion, the cost of private consumption and of private saving and investment. The amount of both should decline, at least relative to what they would have been in the absence of the tax, and again in equal proportion, other things being equal. Moreover, so too would the amount of private employment of labor services fall and in the same proportion as the reduction in capital services, since, as shown above, the VAT would not alter the relative costs of labor and capital inputs. In sum, the imposition of the VAT should result in a reduction of private sector output, at least relative to what it would have been in the tax-free economy. Of course, this reduction is precisely the objective of taxation, i.e., to increase the cost of private uses of production capability relative to public uses in order to reallocate resources from the private to the public sector. To repeat, a VAT would raise the costs of both consumption and saving, and of both capital services and labor services, in equal proportion.

It is this neutrality of the impact of the VAT which should chiefly commend it as the principal tax in our revenue system. By the same token, it is this neutral impact which is the principal basis for advocating the substitution of the VAT for the present income taxation of business.

Compared with the present corporation income tax, the VAT would indeed impose far less of a tax burden on private capital formation. The corporation income tax is an extremely high-rate, selective excise on the use of equity capital in corporate enterprises. It is, moreover, an incremental burden on saving and investment, since the individual income tax itself is biased against saving and for consumption by virtue of the fact that saving is included in the tax base. Substituting the VAT for the corporation income tax, while retaining the other taxes in the federal, state and local fiscal systems, would not eliminate the anti-capital bias in the total revenue scheme, but it would greatly mitigate the additional differential tax burden on capital imposed by the corporate tax. In this respect, therefore, the substitution would represent a major contribution to constructive tax reform.

Substituting the VAT for the corporation income tax would substantially reduce—though not eliminate—the excess cost of using capital services compared with labor services. Reducing the relative cost of capital services would result in an increase in the amount of such services employed with any amount of labor services. Moreover, with a greater rate of private capital formation, the total stock of capital in the private sector would not only be larger but on the average newer and more technologically advanced as well. As a consequence, assuming the law of diminishing returns has not been repealed, labor's productivity and real earnings would be greater than under the present tax system.

The introduction of the VAT as a means of raising additional revenues, rather than as a substitute for existing business taxes, would increase the cost of capital and labor services. Other things being equal, this policy would retard the increase in employment of both labor and capital inputs. Compared with an increase in the corporation income tax rates in order to raise the same amount of additional revenue, however, the VAT would have a more moderate impact on capital formation.

6. The VAT and the Balance of Payments

Much is made by many VAT advocates of the so-called border tax adjustments which are associated with the VAT, i.e., the imposition of the VAT on imports and the rebate of the tax on exports. Ostensibly, these border tax adjustments would increase the prices of imported goods and reduce the prices of exports. Presumably, this change in relative prices would result in a reduction in imports and an increase in exports, hence an increase in the trade surplus (or reduction in the trade deficit).

Upon closer examination, however, the effects of the border tax adjustments are uncertain. They would depend on a number of factors, including whether the VAT were substituted for existing business income taxes, whether monetary and fiscal policies were set so as to preclude an increase in the general level of prices, and the degree of specialization of U.S. exports and imports. For example, assume that monetary-fiscal policy holds the price level unchanged and that the VAT is introduced as a substitute for the present income tax on business profits. Further assume that substantial amounts of U.S. exports are relatively nonspecialized in the sense that exported goods are also produced for U.S. domestic markets, face close substitutes in international markets, and represent a relatively small fraction of the total of such goods traded in these markets. On these assumptions the tax should result in a prompt improvement in the balance of trade. This improvement would result, on the export side, from the fact that export business would become more profitable because of the general exemption of exports from the value added tax. This increased profitability would induce a shift from domestic to foreign sales by the producers of those goods which are not highly specialized in one or the other market. To the extent that our exports encounter close substitutes and are a relatively small fraction of total sales in the world market, U.S. export producers would have no reason to cut the prices of their exports. Increased volume, not price cuts, therefore would be the route to increased export sales revenue.

On the import side, the tax substitution would result in a relative price advantage for import-competing goods domestically produced. This advantage arises from the fact that import prices would rise by the amount of the value added tax imposed on them as they entered the U.S., while prices of domestically produced goods would remain unchanged. The effect on the total value of imports would depend on the elasticity of U.S. demand for imports with respect to their prices, which in turn would depend on the degree of specialization of imports.

If we assume that both our exports and imports are highly specialized, the substitution of value added for corporate income taxation would require a longer period of time to affect the trade account in our balance of payments. As in the former case, the rebate of the value added tax on exports would increase the profitability of the export business. Unless there were excess capacity in export production, however, there would be no reason to reduce export prices. Increases in export volume would occur only as additional production capacity was built up, a time-consuming process. Much the same would be true on the import side. The imposition of the tax on imports would raise their prices relative to domestically produced goods and afford, thereby, an incentive for some reallocation of production capability to import-competing goods. Again, this reallocation would take time.

Next assume that the VAT is adopted not as a substitute for existing taxes but as a source of additional revenue and that the domestic price level rises by the amount of the tax. On these assumptions the imposition of the VAT on imports would not alter the relative prices of imports and of domestically produced import-competing products, nor would the rebate of the tax on exports result in a reduction of export prices compared with their level prior to the adoption of the VAT. Hence, the border tax adjustments would have no immediate impact on the trade account. However, profit margins on export production would be increased relative to those on domestic sales, and some reallocation of output and production capacity to exports would occur. As before, the speed of this adjustment would depend in large part on the degree of specialization of exports.

While these alternative assumptions do not exhaust the possibilities, they do illustrate the cautions required in establishing the impact on the balance of trade of the VAT with border tax adjustments. It may well be that some VAT advocates attribute too much to these border tax adjustments for the short run, just as some observers and policy makers may have counted too heavily on the near-term benefits for our trade balance of the realignment of exchange rates.

Be that as it may, substitution of the VAT for the corporation income tax should in the long run result in important changes in the balance of payments. In the last analysis, any country's trade balance depends on its real comparative advantage in production, hence on the productivity of its production inputs. The productivity gains associated with replacing the corporation income tax by the VAT, therefore, should contribute to improving the trade balance.

A further effect of the substitution should be seen on capital account. Since the U.S. corporation income tax is a very high-rate excise on equity capital, and since the base of the VAT is far larger, the rate of the VAT required to replace corporation income tax revenues is much lower than the corporate tax rate. The substitution, accordingly, would greatly reduce the effective rate of taxation on the returns to equity capital. It is surely reasonable to expect that the increase in after-tax returns would attract foreign investors and induce U.S. investors to allocate more of their capital to domestic enterprises. This change would be only a one-shot effect but possibly of large magnitude.

7. Concluding Comments

Much of the analysis in this discussion has been framed in the context of the VAT as an alternative to the present income taxes on business. For purposes of elucidating the nature of the VAT and its economic impact, this is a useful and appropriate mode of exposition. Moreover, many of the analytical propositions presented above are unaffected by assuming that the VAT would be adopted not as a substitute for, but in lieu of, an increase in present taxes.

The current discussions of the VAT are in a context of enormous deficits in the federal budget, with little prospect, given the present trends in spending and taxes, for their substantial reduction in the near future. Regrettable as it is in the judgment of many economists, it appears that the VAT is more likely to be proposed as a means of obtaining additional revenues than as a substitute for all or part of existing taxes.

If in fact expenditure growth cannot be curbed or if that growth is desired by a majority of the citizens, then it will be necessary to face up honestly to the desirability of increasing taxes. Our examination of the VAT suggests that, given the other objectives and criteria of public financial policy, it would be better to rely on the VAT for the desired additional revenues than to increase any of the existing taxes in the federal revenue system. If the overall effective rate of taxes on the private sector's income must be increased, the VAT would be the least damaging means of doing so.

Technical Note: Calculation of the VAT Base in 1971

The VAT base is readily derived in alternative calculations from the national income accounts (NIA).[12] Four methods are shown in the tables below. The first begins with gross national product, a measure of the total value added in all sectors of the economy, and adjusts this total for those components of GNP which, it is assumed, would be excluded from the VAT base. The second method begins with the NIA estimates of value added in the private sector of the economy. The third starts with national income, a measure of the total payments for factors of production and adjusts this total (a) to exclude such payments made in the government sector, as well as capital outlays, and (b) to add back capital consumption allowances and existing excises, sales, and other so-called indirect business taxes. The last method consists of value added in consumption goods and services plus that in private sector output sold to federal, state, and local governments, less value added originating in households and institutions.

In all of the calculations, value added originating in the government and household sectors of the economy is excluded. As a corollary to the exclusion of the household sector, one-half of the value added in residential construction is included in the VAT base, on the assumption that one-half of the value of residential construction is accounted for by owner-occupied housing. Since the household sector is assumed to be excluded from the tax, no deduction of outlays by households for residential structures would be allowed. On the

---

[12] Cf. U.S. Department of Commerce, Bureau of Economic Analysis, *Survey of Current Business*, April 1972, pp. 13-15.

other hand, the remaining 50 percent of residential construction is assumed to be rental property, the owners of which would deduct their outlays for property acquisition in computing their VAT liabilities.

	$ Billions
VAT Base Derived from Gross National Product, 1971	
Gross national product	1,046.8
Plus:	
Imports	65.3
	1,112.1
Minus:	
Exports	65.3
GNP originating in government sector	124.0
GNP originating in households and institutions	35.5
Nonresidential fixed investment	108.7
50% of residential structures	20.3
Change in business inventories	2.2
Value added tax base	756.1
VAT Base Derived from Private Sector GNP, 1971	
Private sector GNP	922.7
Plus:	
Imports	65.3
	988.0
Minus:	
Exports	65.3
GNP originating in households and institutions	35.5
Nonresidential fixed investment	108.7
50% of residential structures	20.3
Change in business inventories	2.2
Value added tax base	756.0
VAT Base Derived from National Income, 1971	
National income	851.1
Minus:	
National income originating in:	
Government	124.0
Households and institutions	35.5
	691.6

Plus:
Capital consumption allowances	95.2
Indirect business tax and nontax liabilities	102.1
Business transfer payments	4.3
	893.2

Minus:
Nonresidential fixed investment	108.7
50% of residential structures	20.3
Change in business inventories	2.2
Subsidies less current surplus of gov't enterprises	1.0
Statistical discrepancy	4.9
Value added tax base	756.1

VAT Base Derived from Personal Consumption in GNP, 1971

Personal consumption expenditures	662.1

Plus:
Government purchases from private sector	109.0
50% of residential structures	20.3
	791.4

Minus:
GNP originating in households and institutions	35.5
Value added tax base	755.9